24 Recipes for Action

Text copyright © The National Coaching Foundation 1992

ISBN 0 947850 81 3

First published 1992 by
The National Coaching Foundation
4 College Close, Beckett Park, Leeds LS6 3QH

Designed and produced by
White Line Publishing Services
60 Bradford Road, Stanningley, Leeds LS28 6EF
for the Champion Coaching Project

Design: Mike Long
Cover photographs: Noel Whittall
Other photographs: the National Coaching Foundation Regional Development
Officers and Champion Coaching staff

Printed and bound in Great Britain

AFTER-SCHOOL SPORT

24 Recipes for Action

THE STORY OF CHAMPION COACHING

THE NATIONAL COACHING FOUNDATION

CONTENTS

Introduction

*Champion Coaching —
the Story so Far*

I can't believe it is actually here and working! The kids have been waiting for a project of this kind for some time, and are taking full advantage of it ...

So said Mary Warden when Champion Coaching's first School of Sport began on 30 September 1991 in Ryedale, where Mary is the Scheme Liaison Officer. Her enthusiasm is obvious and infectious, but what exactly is this project, and why was it started?

After-school sport

The background to Champion Coaching is the growing dilemma faced in recent years by everyone concerned with after-school sport for young people in the United Kingdom.

The worlds of physical education and community sport are undergoing enormous changes. In schools, there has been legislation affecting the curriculum, teachers' hours, examinations in physical education, and the local management of schools. This has all necessitated a review of the teacher's role in after-school sport. In community sport and recreation there has been a rapid growth in sports development, the professionalisation of coaching, and the advent of compulsory competitive tendering and national vocational qualifications. It is now more critical than ever before that everyone works in partnership to ensure that *all* young people — whatever their ability levels and aspirations — receive the support they need and deserve. The National Curriculum publication *Physical Education for ages 5 to 16* reinforces this point:

There is undoubtedly a need for much better coordination of all these activities between the different bodies involved. This is essential to ensure that young people are made aware of all the opportunities available, and how to gain access to them. The development of partnerships can also ensure that the best use is made of all the available resources. This includes physical resources both in and out of school, as well as the human resources of teachers, parents, coaches, youth workers, and many others involved in providing young people with opportunities for physical activity.

We have great reserves of talent — and now we have a real opportunity to focus that talent and to get after-school sport *right* at long last. Champion Coaching could be the starting-point for that process. This is our chance to build performance pathways for an increased amateur sporting base, and to produce young sportspeople who will go on to become the coaches, officials and sport administrators of the future — as well as the champions ...

Champion Coaching — the idea is conceived

It all happened fast.

In his move from the Department of the Environment to the Department of Education and Science, the Minister for Sport, Robert Atkins MP, was able to make one million pounds available to British sport. £700,000 of that money was allocated to the National Coaching Foundation through the Sports Council in March 1991 to develop an after-school sport programme bringing together young people and coaches across England.

The essence of Champion Coaching

Champion Coaching did not attempt to take one particular model of after-school sport and to impose it on everyone. Rather, it sought to develop a global strategy to be implemented locally in different ways using existing resources and strengths. England became a nationwide testing ground as Champion Coaching sought to find workable solutions to the many questions which were being posed. They discovered that after-school sport was currently rather like a collection of unplanned roads — some good, some not so good — which did not network effectively together. Champion Coaching is aiming to provide an accurate road map — and to build new link roads so that all children can travel safely and as far as they wish to go.

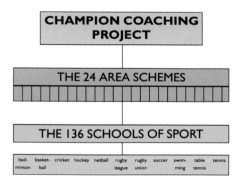

The structure of Champion Coaching
Each of the twenty-four area schemes covered several (but not all) of the eleven sports selected for Champion Coaching.

As well as this overall plan, there are three elements of after-school sport for which Champion Coaching has had responsibility:

1 The Schools of Sport have had to be planned and carried out effectively, as models for future schemes throughout the UK to observe and learn from.

2 Champion Coaching is working to identify the critical ingredients in the complex mix that currently comprises after-school sport. The twenty-four schemes were like a laboratory to test out which ingredients are vital and which recipes work best. Out of this process, we have been able to recommend national strategies on which future projects can be based.

3 We had a day-to-day responsibility to promote the task of coaches working with children. This included being a mediator between national governing bodies of sport and local authorities. We also aimed to be a voice for the concerns of parents, and to help develop opportunities for the children. There have been many participants in the Champion Coaching Project, and the challenge we faced was to balance their input for the long-term benefit of young people in sport.

Champion Coaching fits well into the performance band of the standard sport development model (see the diagram below right on this page). Most of the Schools of Sport were aimed at young-sters who had a little skill and some experience, but who needed access to good coaching in order to develop further. A few squads were for children in the excellence band, but this was not the chief aim.

> *The name 'Champion Coaching' means that we find champion coaches and train them to help young sportspeople achieve their own level of excellence — not necessarily to be future Olympic champions, but to reach their own full potential.*

Making a start

The duration of the project was specified as 1 April 1991 to 31 March 1992. Three key personnel were identified — Katie Donovan, Clive Bond and Karen Rhodes — and the eleven sports to be included in the scheme announced: badminton, basketball, cricket, hockey, netball, rugby league, rugby union, soccer, swimming, table tennis, and tennis.

Katie Donovan, Project Coordinator

No project of this size and complexity could have worked without the right person at the helm. Originally, Katie came from Philadelphia, Pennsylvania, in the United States of America. A keen sports enthusiast as a youngster, Katie went to Springfield College, Springfield, Massachusetts, where she majored in health and physical education. She took time out of her course to spend a year in England at Chelsea College of Physical Education.

Below: Katie Donovan (centre), Clive Bond and Karen Rhodes

Katie taught physical education and coached sport for fifteen years, obtaining a Master's degree in physical education and sports administration and a Certificate of Advanced Study in Sports Administration on the way. Eventually she left teaching and coaching to move into coach education as the Director of the American Coaching Effectiveness Program, one of the divisions of Human Kinetics Publishers, based in Illinois. Katie is currently employed by Sheffield Polytechnic as a senior lecturer to head up their new sports development unit. She has been generously loaned to the National Coaching Foundation for the duration of the Champion Coaching Project.

The standard sport development model (right)
The approximate range covered by Champion Coaching is indicated in red.

Clive Bond, Assistant Coordinator

Clive Bond has an equally impressive and varied history of involvement in sport. A former soccer and cricket player, he graduated to become an FA and NCA staff coach. After teaching physical education in schools, he went into teacher training, lecturing at Jordanhill and Loughborough, and became head of Carnegie in 1976.

Since his retirement in 1986, Clive has been closely involved with the National Coaching Foundation, organising conferences and working on international liaison, particularly with the International Olympic Committee.

Karen Rhodes, Project Administrator

Karen came to the National Coaching Foundation from being a qualified medical secretary. She became the Personal Assistant to the Director, and was transferred to Champion Coaching because of her knowledge and enthusiasm.

Ambitious plans

Meeting people

One of the essential features of Champion Coaching has been to build bridges between all the agencies and people involved in after-school sport — the Sports Councils, the national governing bodies, clubs, local authorities, schools, physical education teachers, and coaches.

The first round of meetings was held with the regional directors of the ten Sports Council regions in England, many of whom were already involved in after-school sport projects. Champion Coaching's objective was to build on these examples of good practice as well as to develop appropriate new initiatives. Meetings were

also held with the other key players in the team: the British Council of Physical Education, the Central Council of Physical Recreation, the National Council for Schools Sports, and the eleven national governing bodies of sport who were to be part of the project.

The timescale for Champion Coaching was very tight, but we were determined above all that every aspect of the project would be of high quality. Criteria were therefore established and published. These can be summarised as follows:

- The schemes were limited to England, for practical reasons; follow-up schemes, however, could well embrace the rest of the United Kingdom.
- They had to be capable of providing the Schools of Sport during the period mid-October to mid-December 1991.

- The schemes had to adhere to the philosophy and ethos of Champion Coaching. In the short term, this means giving all the children a great experience of sport. In the longer term, the schemes had to contribute to the goal of bringing agencies together and working towards a national strategy for after-school sport.
- Above all, they had to provide high-quality coaching.
- They had to operate within a realistic and affordable budget.
- Each scheme had to nominate a competent professional as Scheme Liaison Officer.

Promoting the project

Once Champion Coaching got under way, publicity material was required. First the now-familiar oval logo was designed. Then White Line Publishing Services were commissioned to produce an information leaflet, setting out the basics of the project, and a wall poster designed to encourage schoolchildren to get involved.

To maintain the flow of information, Champion Coaching has published a regular newsletter. This has been distributed to an ever-wider circulation list, including MPs, the press, and those involved in sport at grass-roots level — coaches, teachers, parents.

The SportLogs

With so many different people involved in after-school sport, it is critical for each child to retain a sense of personal direction and progress.

In an attempt to help them to do this and to record their experiences of Champion Coaching, a loose-leaf publication was devised. These *SportLogs* were the personal property of each child, but at certain points coaches, teachers and parents were encouraged to be actively involved.

At the back of each *SportLog* there were three sheets on which the children recorded their own honest responses to the project. These were collected by the coaches and sent to the Champion Coaching monitoring team for analysis and evaluation.

Some of the comments made by the children on the *SportLog* response sheets are reproduced in the panel.

Comments from the children

What attracted you to Champion Coaching?
- *I wanted to improve my hockey skills and everything with a proper coach*
- *Because I like cricket and I thought I could meet new friends and get better at cricket*

How were you picked for Champion Coaching?
- *I think because I am quite enthusiastic because even if I get hurt I still keep playing my best*
- *Through the club really and by hassling Ms Kraus*

If you enjoyed it, please tell us why
- *Because I met new friends and learned new skills*
- *I got lots of exercise and my Dad watched me*
- *We had the chance of being coached by top-class coaches*

Any other comments?
- *The warm-ups were boring*
- *There should be more of them for people to learn to like sports*
- *My mother couldn't read my SportLog!*

It all begins to happen!

It is one thing to make plans and to draw up criteria, but another to turn them into reality. Fortunately no one had to go out to trawl for schemes — the problem was quite the opposite. The response was tremendous: 120 proposals came in from a wide range of agencies. Of these, 36 schemes were shortlisted, and Katie Donovan, along with regional officers of the Sports Council, interviewed them all over a period of four weeks.

In the end 24 schemes were chosen. The majority were conventional, with links to the local authority and the regional Sports Council, but there were exceptions. Two examples illustrate this: the London Playing Fields Society scheme is not linked to any of the standard agencies of after-school sport, but nonetheless has all the avenues needed to make it work. The Hampshire Active Partners scheme is county-wide, but with no local-authority involvement: the links are direct to the schools, which are operating under LMS (Local Management of Schools), and which already had a good working relationship with the regional Sports Council.

Training the coaches

It's not only the children who got a great deal out of Champion Coaching — the coaches did too! Most coaches in Britain are volunteers who work in their own time and often at their own expense to support the development of young sportspeople.

Selection

The selection of the head coaches was a joint enterprise between the national governing bodies of sport and the Scheme Liaison Officers, as indeed it had to be if it was to be a meaningful partnership:

● The governing bodies drafted the criteria for the coaches in each sport, in terms of formal coaching qualifications, experience in coaching children and commitment to their own continuing professional development.

● These criteria were approved by Champion Coaching headquarters, who ensured that they were reasonably consistent across the different sports.

● The Scheme Liaison Officers then nominated the coaches they wanted; in some cases these were selected from a list supplied by the governing body.

● The governing bodies and Champion Coaching approved their choice.

The residential training weekends

Once the head coaches were appointed, they were sent various distance-learning materials in preparation for the training weekends. These included the relevant National Coaching Foundation resource material at introductory and key-course level, the pack that the parents were given at the 'Young People in Sport' workshops (see page 11), the *CoachLog* (a companion to the *SportLog*, which guided the coaches through what they had to do during the Schools of Sport), and some sport-specific resource material recommended by the national governing bodies.

There were three residential weekends:

1 13–15 September, Loughborough University: hockey, soccer, rugby union, tennis.

2 20–22 September, Crystal Palace National Sports Centre: rugby league, swimming, netball, badminton.

3 27–29 September, Lilleshall National Sports Centre: table tennis, cricket, basketball.

All three weekends consisted of the same programme. On Friday evening there was an introduction to the philosophy and structure of the Champion Coaching project. Then on Saturday two of the National Coaching Foundation staff tutors, Mr Rod Thorpe (Physical Education and Sports Science Department, Loughborough University) and Dr Martin Lee (Institute for the Study of Children in Sports, Bedford College of Higher Education), took the coaches through relevant National Coaching Foundation key courses. Finally on Sunday the national governing bodies took their own coaches through sport-specific workshops.

It was very intensive, but the coaches found it worthwhile and stimulating — if exhausting! The monitoring team (see page 12) reviewed the weekend and examined the reactions to it.

What the coaches said

• *The best thing I ever attended*

• *It really helped me to feel good about myself as a coach of young people.*

• *I didn't realise how much I didn't know — I understand Champion Coaching much better now.*

• *It was terrific to come together with other Champion Coaching coaches. Now I really see that this is a national project and we form a team.*

Overall the weekends were very encouraging: the commitment, enthusiasm and professionalism of the coaches bodes well for the future.

Final preparations

Selecting the children

This was perhaps the key step in organising the project.

During the planning stages, it had been estimated that about 4,000 children would be involved. In the event, at least 6,000 took part — an achievement that speaks for itself.

In the initial discussions, the Scheme Liaison Officers were given general guidance on how the children should be selected. The normal method was as follows:

● The Scheme Liaison Officer met with the heads of physical education at the selected schools, and set out the age-group of the children, the sports, the coaches, the facilities and transport details.

● The Scheme Liaison Officer then asked the heads of physical education, armed with this information, to draw up criteria for the squads. These invariably included a commitment to sport, a healthy attitude, a degree of responsibility, and a basic minimum level of skill and performance.

● The criteria were then adjusted and fine-tuned in the light of local circumstances.

● Then the physical education teachers in each participating school were asked to nominate a certain number of children. The Scheme Liaison Officer took the top 75 per cent of these, leaving the remainder on the reserve list in case some children dropped out at a later stage.

The method described above was the usual one, but there were some exceptions. In areas where the rapport with schools or physical education teachers was less effective, children were recruited by advertising the scheme in clubs, leisure centres, churches, and other places where young people go.

The PE roadshow

This was a travelling roadshow about Champion Coaching which visited each of the 24 schemes during September and October. The Champion Coaching

headquarters team led the roadshow, which was intended for teachers who had been involved in helping to select the children for the schemes. The idea was to explain Champion Coaching from a national perspective, to encourage teachers to support its concept and aims, and to raise more general issues about after-school sport.

These roadshows had a mixed reception. The numbers attending varied, and the concerns raised reflected the low morale of the profession at the present time. There was clearly a need to reaffirm the crucial role that physical education teachers play in the development of sport for school-age children and to reassure them that Champion Coaching does have a strong educational basis.

The National Confederation of Parent–Teacher Associations

One of the most useful new links formed by Champion Coaching was with the National Confederation of Parent–Teacher Associations, a huge organisation which has over 8,500 constituent PTAs. The NCPTA was keen to support the work of Champion Coaching and to distribute information about it to its members.

It is hoped that the NCPTA may decide officially to approve the materials that the National Coaching Foundation is developing for the education of parents, first drafts of which were used in the 'Young People in Sport' workshops (see page 11).

The NCPTA was also able to help some schemes in a practical way. For example, if a Scheme Liaison Officer rang Champion Coaching headquarters with an unexpected transport problem, we could contact the local PTA and ask them to help out by arranging a 'parent pool' of drivers. Seeing that the project was worthwhile, they were enthusiastic and glad to respond to such a challenge.

The Schools of Sport

The Schools of Sport were the core of Champion Coaching. They were the vehicles for bringing the skills of the coaches to the children. The first one started in Ryedale on 30 September, and the last one finished in Northamptonshire on 20 December. Most Schools of Sport lasted for six to eight weeks, although many schemes have expanded to include extra sessions.

It is not necessary to describe the Schools of Sport in detail here, as each scheme is fully covered in the Scheme-by-Scheme Review on pages 13–63. Suffice it to say that the problems have been ones of success and enthusiasm. Some schemes took on more children than originally envisaged, and more T-shirts and SportLogs somehow had to be found. Some Scheme Liaison Officers found they had a problem with transport, and had to ring up to ask for help. But on the whole everything went surprisingly smoothly.

The Schools of Sport received a number of visits from VIPs and the media. The

Minister for Sport attended a number of sessions, as did staff from the Sports Council. Newspapers, local radio and television also featured the schemes on a number of occasions.

Keeping a record

There are three main ways in which the Schools of Sport have been recorded for posterity.

First, the children have recorded what they have done in their SportLogs, and these are of continuing value to themselves as well as to their coaches, teachers and parents.

Second, the Scheme Liaison Officers have kept careful notes of all aspects of their schemes, and have used these to fill in questionnaires which were sent back to Champion Coaching headquarters. It is the facts reported in these questionnaires that have formed the basis for this book.

Third, the National Coaching Foundation Regional Development Officers were entrusted with the task of taking reproduction-quality photographs of the schemes in their area. Where necessary, they were loaned suitable cameras and given specific guidance on how to achieve the standard required.

Who gets what from Champion Coaching?

The children

Champion Coaching is above all for the children. Those taking part get a great deal:

- The chief benefit is a highly qualified coach who has been trained, selected and approved — an enormous plus.
- The best possible facilities and equipment were made available for the scheme.
- In most cases, transport to and from the Schools of Sport was provided.
- A SportLog to record their experiences of Champion Coaching.
- A Champion Coaching T-shirt.
- Fair play education, leading to the Champion Coaching Fair Play Award certificate and a Fair Play sweatshirt (see page 11).

The head coaches

In addition to the kudos of taking part, the 136 head coaches also received some significant benefits from Champion Coaching:

● The three-day residential training weekend, with all their travel expenses paid.

● Champion Coaching kit: sports bag, tracksuit, sports shirt, training shoes.

● A complete set of resource materials for distance-learning about working with children.

● A voucher, valid for a year, for the National Coaching Foundation Advanced Workshop on first aid.

● A free Coaching Focus Gold subscription for a year, with the coaching insurance boosted from the standard £1 million to £2 million cover.

● An invitation to the Coach of the Year Fair Play Award ceremony.

● A payment of £200 to cover their travel and subsistence costs during the scheme.

The assistant coaches

In virtually every case, the assistant coaches were paid a realistic hourly rate which reflected normal commercial pay in the area. Usually this came from the Scheme Liaison Officer's budget, but sometimes the cost was met by the local authority.

Within the existing budgets and timescale, it was regrettably not possible to give the 320 or so assistant coaches a package of benefits similar to those which the head coaches received. However, their contribution was highly valued — indeed, it was vital for the success of the project.

Follow-up

The 'Young People in Sport' workshops

These 24 workshops — one per scheme — were held during October and November, roughly at the same time as the Schools of Sport. The idea was to invite all the parents of the children involved in Champion Coaching, and to raise their awareness of their role in supporting their children's involvement in sport.

A member of the Champion Coaching headquarters team ran the workshops, assisted by the head coaches of the schemes. They opened with an introduction illustrated with overhead transparencies, which led into small-group discussions followed by a closing presentation. At the end of the evening, all the parents were given three National Coaching Foundation publications — *The Playsport Guide* (an audio tape plus booklet), *Fair Play for Children in Sport*, and *Working with Children*.

The 'exit schemes'

From day one it was realised that Champion Coaching must not stop dead when the Schools of Sport finished. There had to be easy routes for the children to follow, to continue their involvement with sport and good coaching.

These exit schemes were not centrally planned, but devised by the local Scheme Liaison Officers. As it has turned out, they have achieved much more than was first envisaged. Links with local clubs have been central, but in some cases extra sessions have been provided as extensions of Champion Coaching itself. Perhaps the most impressive example is in Bury St Edmunds, where a ten-year plan has been developed covering all age-groups, of which Champion Coaching has become the sector for the 11–14s.

Already there are exciting opportunities for children growing out of the first Champion Coaching programme, and that alone has made it worthwhile.

Coach education follow-up days

While aiming to provide high-quality coaching, it was never intended to bring in coaches from outside each area. In practice many of the Champion Coaching coaches came from the same locality as the schemes where they were working.

However, it was decided to go one step further — to try to leave each area with a better coaching legacy than before Champion Coaching began, by drawing new potential coaches in.

To achieve this, a coach education follow-up day was held in each of the 24 scheme areas. Those invited were parents, volunteer helpers, and indeed everyone who had shown some interest in coaching as a result of the scheme. The

NCF Regional Development Officers organised these days. Those who came were introduced to the basic principles of coaching, and were encouraged to get involved and become qualified.

Of course, the new coaches who have been recruited through these days need to be put to work. So the Scheme Liaison Officers, or their successors, will be looking to appoint them as assistant coaches when the opportunity arises.

The Fair Play Awards

The principles of fair play and sportsmanship are central to the ethos of Champion Coaching, and it was decided early on to make an award to one young player in each School of Sport in recognition of his or her achievement in

this area. We were delighted when this initiative was endorsed by Mrs Jean Pickering in memory of her late husband. The awards are now known as the Ron Pickering Memorial Fund Fair Play Awards.

Fair Play Award Certificates and Champion Coaching sweatshirts were awarded to 136 children. Two of these award-winners — one boy and one girl — were invited (with their parents) to a luncheon and award ceremony at the Café Royal in London on 17 December. All 136 head coaches were invited to the ceremony, which was combined with the British Institute of Sports Coaches annual Coach of the Year awards presentation, rounding off the project with a public recognition of what all outstanding coaches can achieve.

Above: *Windsor Fair Play Award winner Catriona Greenshields with badminton coach Bob Reed*

Bouquets and brickbats

Monitoring and evaluation

Every project, particularly one like Champion Coaching with a sizeable budget, needs to be monitored to make sure it is delivering the goods and providing value for money.

There were two forms of review undertaken in Champion Coaching: consultation and formal monitoring.

In order to reach an overview of the project and its implications for the future, review meetings were held with the key agencies:

4–5 December 1991
Scheme Liaison Officers

8–9 January 1992
Sports Council senior regional officers

15 January 1992
National governing bodies of sport

23 January 1992
BCPE, SCOPE, PEA, BAALPE

The formal monitoring was a fully independent external evaluation carried out by a team of three: Phyl Edwards, who is an independent consultant, Malcolm Tungate, the Sports Council research officer responsible for monitoring all the Council's projects for young people, and Debbie McDonald, also from the Sports Council. A full monitoring and evaluation report will be produced.

Reporting back

There are many people throughout British sport who are very keen to hear what has happened in Champion Coaching and to learn the lessons from it. We are reporting in three ways:

1 This book, *24 Recipes for Action*, tells the story of Champion Coaching and highlights the results and lessons to be learned. It should prove useful in many practical ways to those involved in similar projects in future years.

2 The National Coaching Foundation Annual Conference for 1992, held on 11 March, will be devoted entirely to after-school sport, under the theme 'Champion Coaching — a pattern for progress'. The programme is divided into various 'chapters', introduced by speakers with specialist knowledge. The Conference is being promoted to attract a much wider range of people than those who regularly come to National Coaching Foundation conferences. It will provide a useful opportunity to discuss the issues arising out of Champion Coaching, directly reaching the ears of some of the most important decision-makers in sport.

24 Recipes for Action is being published simultaneously with the conference, and a copy will be included in each conference pack. Also, each of the twenty-four schemes has been given the opportunity to set up a display showing what they have done.

3 A full official report on Champion Coaching will be produced in due course, giving exhaustive details of all that happened, including a final account of how the resources were raised and used.

December 1991

Scheme-by-Scheme Review

Using the scheme-by-scheme review

The 24 Scheme Liaison Officers have supplied us with information about their schemes by filling in questionnaires. For ease of comparison, we have distilled all this into a standard format. In some cases it was necessary to abridge the information slightly to save space. Wherever possible, we have quoted the Scheme Liaison Officer's comments on the scheme.

The locations of the schemes are shown on the map opposite. For a key to the scheme numbers, please see the panel on the right of this page. The schemes are numbered and listed in alphabetical order.

For ease of use, this section has been designed so that the description of each scheme occupies a double-page spread. First comes the address and contact details for the Scheme Liaison Officer; then an introductory paragraph briefly describing the scheme, set in larger *italic* type; and then the detailed data listings.

Most of the sections are self-explanatory, but these comments may be helpful:

The coaches

Normally the ratio of coaches:children is calculated by the straightforward formula (head coaches + assistant coaches)/children. However, in some cases — particularly where one head coach dealt with more than one squad — this would have given a misleading impression, and the ratio has been adjusted accordingly.

The Schools of Sport

We have not given the exact times at which all the Schools of Sport were held, as this would have been too complex. Instead we have indicated into which of three broad categories they fell:

● after school (up to 6:00 pm)
● evening (6:00 pm onwards)
● weekends

Management structure

The block diagrams indicate the 'chain of command' leading to the Champion Coaching Schools of Sport. There were many variations, and no attempt has been made to force this information into a standard format. The role of Champion Coaching headquarters has been assumed, and therefore, with one exception, has not been shown. The exception is Bristol, where Champion Coaching's management role was unusually direct.

Other agencies involved

The following agencies were involved in virtually all the schemes, and so have not been listed each time:

● The National Coaching Foundation
● NCF National Coaching Centres
● The Sports Councils (including regional and local)
● Local authorities
● Sports development officers
● Schools
● Local sports clubs who provided facilities and exit routes

Funding

The primary funding of each scheme was an individually negotiated grant from Champion Coaching central office. Some schemes managed to attract additional funding, and this is mentioned, as is any revenue generated by charging the children.

The Scheme Liaison Officer's time was normally provided free of charge by his or her employer, who was generally the 'major partner' in the scheme. Sometimes other functions, such as administration or advertising and promotion, were also provided free.

The local expenditure of each scheme has been allocated to six standard categories, and shown in the form of a pie chart with percentages indicated. The category 'coaches' refers to expenditure on assistant coaches, as the head coaches were funded centrally. The nature of the expenditure in the 'other' category is given where known.

Scope for development

The Scheme Liaison Officers' comments on local development are recorded in this section. Many of them also commented on the general scope for development of Champion Coaching nationally, and their views have been taken into account in Chapter 4 (pages 73–77).

Key to the schemes

1 ACCESS (Active Champion Coaching for Eastbourne Schools' Sport)
2 Blackburn Champion Coaching in association with South Ribble
3 Bradford Champion Coaching
4 Bristol Champion Coaching
5 Bromley Champion Coaching
6 Champion Coaching with the Sports Training Scheme (Notts.)
7 Chelmsford Champion Coaching
8 Cheshire Champion Coaching
9 Coventry Champion Coaching
10 Derby Champion Coaching
11 Ealing Champion Coaching
12 Hampshire Active Partners Champion Coaching
13 London Playing Fields Society — Champion Coaching
14 Middlesbrough Champion Coaching
15 Northamptonshire Champion Coaching
16 Peterborough Champion Coaching
17 RACE (Ryedale Active Coaching Experience)
18 Sheffield Champion Coaching
19 Shropshire Champion Coaching
20 STEP (Sports Training towards Excellence and Performance)
21 St Edmundsbury Champion Choice
22 Surrey Champion Coaching
23 The Three Cs (Carlisle Champion Coaching)
24 Windsor and Maidenhead Champion Coaching

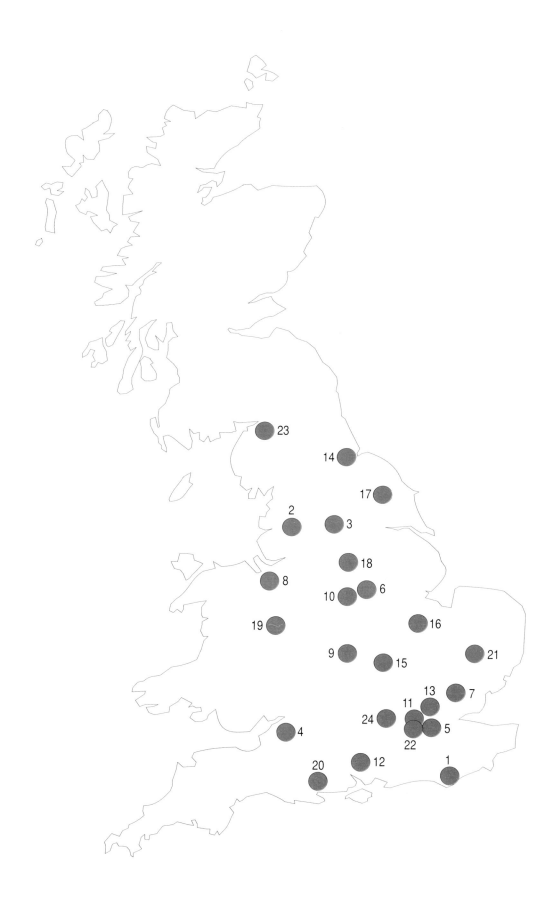

Scheme 1

ACCESS (Active Champion Coaching for Eastbourne Schools' Sport)

Scheme Liaison Officer: Robert Lake
Job title: East Sussex County Sports
    Development Officer
Scheme address:
Chelsea School of Human Movement
Hillbrow Cottage
Gaudick Road
Eastbourne
East Sussex
BN20 7SP
Telephone: 0273 643761

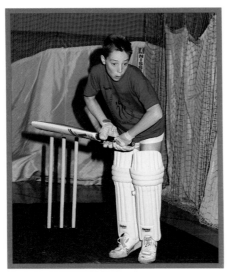

The lessons learned from Sportslink — a similar initiative to Champion Coaching, launched in Brighton and Hove in February 1988 — made it clear that the schools and clubs would support ACCESS with real commitment if they received assurances that it would be a long-term scheme rather than a flash in the pan. It would mean that many more children would gain access to the Schools of Sport and that sufficient time would be available to encourage local clubs to start junior or colts sections where they did not exist. ACCESS will therefore continue until July 1992.

The Schools of Sport

The Schools of Sport ran once a week for six weeks, are still continuing, and are planned to do so until July 1992. All except two took place at the weekend.

Children enrolled	152
Number of sessions	6
Potential attendances	912
Actual attendances	680
Percentage attendance	**75%**

Recruiting the children

The children were recruited through the head coaches and the PE departments of the five participating schools. The Scheme Liaison Officer visited the schools on many occasions and explained what sort of children were being sought.

Choosing the children

Sport	Selection criteria
All	Those not currently involved with clubs who would be reliable and show commitment.

How the scheme was managed

Major partners: East Sussex County Council
Project managers: Robert Lake and Sue Law (Coordinator, Eastbourne National Coaching Centre).

The Scheme Liaison Officer is employed by East Sussex County Council. *Time spent on project:* 12–15 hours per week. Sue Law spent one day per week on the project also.

Other agencies involved

Chelsea School of Human Movement

Management structure

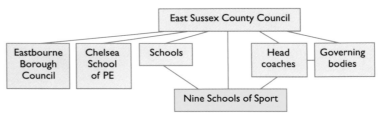

The children

Sport	Sex	Age group	Ability level
Badminton	Mixed	13–15	Foundation/participation
Basketball	Mixed	12–15	Foundation/participation
	Mixed	12–15	Performance/excellence
Cricket	Mixed	13–15	Foundation/participation
Hockey	Mixed	13–15	Foundation/participation
Netball	Girls	13–15	Foundation/participation
Soccer	Girls	10–12	Foundation/participation
	Girls	13–15	Foundation/participation
Tennis	Mixed	13–15	Foundation/participation

The coaches

Sport	No. children in squad	Head coaches	Assistant coaches	Ratio of coaches:children
Badminton	16	1	2	1:5
Basketball	11	1	2	1:4
	17	1	2	1:6
Cricket	14	1	1	1:7
Hockey	17	1	2	1:6
Netball	28	1	4	1:5
Soccer	25	1	3	1:6
Tennis	24	1	3	1:6

About the coaches

Two head coaches and five assistant coaches were PE teachers.

Payment per hour for assistant coaches: none. Instead, the scheme promised to provide a free coach education package, a track suit and whole or part payment of fees for courses leading to governing body awards.

Minimum qualifications for assistant coaches: a leader's award. We also stipulated that they had to attend a coach education session presented by the National Coaching Foundation. If we had asked for a higher qualification, I doubt whether we would have found the required number of assistant coaches.

Extra training provided: see above.

Transport

Transport was arranged informally.

Promoting the scheme

The scheme was publicised in schools through headteachers, heads of year and PE departments. Articles about the scheme appeared in the local press. Additionally, clubs and coaches were approached via the local Sports Council. Coaches were also recruited via county sports associations and from the student body at Chelsea School of Human Movement.

We held an official launch to which were invited county councillors, borough councillors, representatives of the Leisure and Recreation Department, the local Sports Council, the county PE Adviser, headteachers, governors, PE teachers, the press, the head and assistant coaches and the South East Council for Sport.

Twenty-eight parents attended the 'Young People in Sport' workshop and a small number came to watch the coaching sessions.

Additional funding

Contribution from children: A fee of 50p per session (£1.00 for tennis) was charged. However, it was made clear to the schools that fees should be waived for children experiencing hardship. The total collected was £476.

How the money was spent

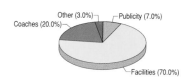

Coaches (20.0%)
Other (3.0%)
Publicity (7.0%)
Facilities (70.0%)

Administration: covered within the East Sussex County Council Sports Development budget. *Other expenses:* Scheme Liaison Officer travel expenses.

Strengths of the scheme

- All the coaches demonstrated a very high level of commitment to the scheme. They cared a great deal about what they were trying to achieve, and particularly about the children.

- Support from Chelsea School for Human Movement, East Sussex County Council, some clubs (but too few), Sussex County Cricket Club, the National Coaching Foundation Regional Development Officer, and the local press.

- In the main, the Schools of Sport were well attended; the kids were great.

- Good facilities and support staff at each of the sites.

- Liaison with schools.

- The efforts of all involved!

Weaknesses

- There were communication problems before the Schools of Sport between head coaches and their assistants, mainly due to the late identification of the assistants. Communication was also difficult between the Scheme Liaison Officer and the head coaches, not helped by the fact that the SLO was living in London at the time.

- Identification and involvement of local assistant coaches.

- Those clubs which wished to become involved were supportive and saw the value of having a junior section. Unfortunately these clubs were too few.

- The Eastbourne Sports Council expressed support, but very little was forthcoming.

Competition

Some competition was included within the Schools of Sport. It was designed to be enjoyable and to indicate what each child had learned during the six-week period.

Problems with other agencies

We didn't have any great problems, but there was a degree of indifference from most clubs and from one or two schools.

Scope for development

I would like the scheme to be expanded into other areas of East Sussex using existing borough and district council leisure departments and Sports Development Officers.

A ten-minute video, posters and literature will be presented to the National

Westminster Bank, the Sports Council, and county, borough and district councils to gain sponsorship. A submission to the National Foundation for Sport and the Arts is also intended.

The long-term intention is for ACCESS to become Active Champion Coaching for East Sussex Schools. This will require not only further funding on a much larger scale, but also the consolidation of the existing sports network so that the scheme can be delivered effectively.

Other comments

The scheme has been a valuable experience, particularly for me. It has demonstrated the need for structured provision of extra-curricular sport, and will help me to avoid making some thankfully not-too-serious mistakes again in the future.

The facilities

Sport	Facility	Owned by	Hourly hire rate
Badminton	Sports hall (leisure centre)	Eastbourne Borough Council	£ 7.80
Basketball	Gymnasium (school)	East Sussex County Council	Free
Cricket	Sports hall (leisure centre)	Eastbourne Borough Council	£ 7.80
Hockey	Redgra / playing fields	Chelsea Sch'l of Human Movement	£13.04
Netball	Sports hall (leisure centre)	Eastbourne Borough Council	£10.00
Soccer	Playing field	Chelsea Sch'l of Human Movement	£10.00
Tennis	Courts	David Lloyd Racket Centre	£32.50 (4 c'ts)

Scheme

2

Blackburn Champion Coaching in association with South Ribble

Scheme Liaison Officer: Chris Hughes
Job title: Community Recreation Officer
Scheme address:
East Park Lodge
East Park Road
Blackburn
BB1 8DW
Telephone: 0254 585238

The Schools of Sport

The Schools of Sport ran once a week over a six-week period. Half took place after school and half in the early evening.

Children enrolled	176
Number of sessions	6
Potential attendances	1032
Actual attendances	1008
Percentage attendances	**98%**

Recruiting the children

In Blackburn, teachers from ten schools were solely responsible for selecting three children from each sport from their school, based on the criteria below.

Selection in South Ribble was more locally based around two schools for each sport, and selection was via liaison with teachers.

Choosing the children

Sport	Selection criteria
Badminton	Those playing at school-team standard.
Netball	Those playing at school-team standard.
Hockey	Those at performance/ participation standard with previous knowledge of the game.
Rugby league	Girls who were beginners.
Rugby union	Boys from non-rugby-playing schools — participation level.

The Blackburn and South Ribble scheme — based around two centres — has given sports coaching in the area the high profile needed to make young participants feel part of something that is a bit special. Our scheme is about forming good communication networks so that the good practice we achieved continues within schools and clubs. It is not only about good-quality coaching, but also about raising the profile of the coaches who have delivered that service, particularly at local level. We will continue the coach education programme so that the young people get the sort of support that will make them tomorrow's responsible players and performers.

The children

Sport	Sex	Age group	Ability level
Badminton	Mixed	14	Participation/performance
Hockey (2 schools)	Mixed	11–12	Participation/performance
Netball (2 schools)	Girls	12–13	Participation/performance
Rugby league (2 schools)	Girls	13–15	Participation/performance
Rugby union	Boys	14	Participation/performance

The coaches

Sport	No. of children in squad	Head coaches	Assistant coaches	Ratio of coaches:children
Badminton	24	1	3	1:6
Hockey	28 + 28	1	1 + 3	1:9
Netball	30 + 20	1	3 + 3	1:6
Rugby league	12 + 12	1	–	1:12
Rugby union	18	1	2	1:6

How the scheme was managed

Major partner: Blackburn Borough Council in association with South Ribble Borough Council

Project managed by: Blackburn and South Ribble Borough Councils

The Scheme Liaison Officer is employed by Blackburn Borough Council. *Time spent on project:* 5 hours per week.

Management structure

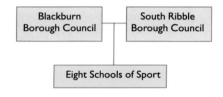

About the coaches

One head coach and three assistant coaches were PE teachers.

Payment per hour for assistant coaches: £10.00

Minimum qualifications for assistant coaches: national governing body preliminary standard.

Extra training provided: some training was given to the assistant coaches by the head coaches.

Transport

All transport was arranged informally by the children's parents and teachers.

Promoting the scheme

Individual contact was made with the schools and clubs involved. Posters and leaflets appeared on the school notice-boards. Children were also informed about the scheme by their teachers.

Parents of selected children were informed by direct mail via their children.

A launch party was held which was attended by the Minister for Sport.

Additional funding

Contribution from children: none

How the money was spent

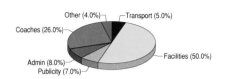

Other expenses: launch party; hot food for Saturday morning rugby.

Strengths of the scheme

● Good coaches. Coaches found us because they were keen to be involved. They did not look upon their involvement in the scheme as just another source of income.

● Good school links, which had already been formed through Sportivation, our own schools liaison project.

● Access to good facilities.

● The ability of the Scheme Liaison Officer to devote time to the project was significant in the success of the Schools of Sport.

Weaknesses

● The time of year at which the Schools of Sport took place. It was beginning to get too cold to hold coaching outside, particularly for the younger children.

● There were too many participating schools. It was hard to limit the teachers to finding only three children per sport from their school.

Competition

It is planned to introduce some internal and some external competition in the future.

New links

Existing links with schools have been strengthened; Champion Coaching has enabled us to contact clubs to offer a major scheme, which previously would have been impractical.

Problems with other agencies

There was an added challenge to publicising this particular scheme given the complex local political situation.

Scope for development

The scheme could be developed by further strengthening links with clubs and by offering incentives for those clubs to offer structured follow-on schemes for the children.

The Blackburn and South Ribble scheme has provided us with a firm base, identifiable by children, schools and clubs, on which to build the future schemes (summer schools, etc.) that we will certainly be promoting.

The facilities

Sport	Facility	Owned by	Hourly hire rate
Badminton	Sports hall (leisure centre)	Blackburn Borough Council	£16.50
Hockey	Sportsturf pitch	Blackburn Borough Council	£18.50
Netball	Sports hall (school)	Lancashire County Council	£16.50
Rugby league	Pitch (leisure centre)	Blackburn Borough Council	£16.50
Rugby union	Pitch (club)	Blackburn Rugby Club	£16.50

Scheme

3

Bradford Champion Coaching

Scheme Liaison Officer: Deiniol Williams
Job title: Project Coordinator — Sport and
    Young People Project
Scheme address:
Recreation Division
2nd Floor
Central House
Forster Square
Bradford
BD1 1DJ
Telephone: 0274 752626

The underlying principles and nature of the Champion Coaching Project are identical to the usual pattern of sports development long ago developed in Bradford, and it was therefore natural for us to become involved in this nationwide project.

The Recreation Division, supported by the Sport and Young People Project, has already used this pattern very successfully with indoor hockey, table tennis and jazz dance.

The Champion Coaching Project gave us the opportunity to apply funding to similar programmes of coaching in six individual sports, especially to provide new and appropriate equipment, transport and an improved ratio of coaches to pupils.

The Schools of Sport

The Schools of Sport ran once a week over a six-week period. They all took place after school.

Children enrolled	164
Number of sessions	6
Potential attendances	984
Actual attendances	879
Percentage attendance	**89%**

Recruiting the children

Letters were sent to schools in July 1991 and follow-up visits were made by the Scheme Liaison Officer and head coaches. Schools were asked to nominate children and reserves (four to six altogether). The selection process was based entirely on the PE teachers' knowledge of the children.

Choosing the children

Sport	Selection criteria
Swimming	Those whose performance at the 1991 Bradford Schools Championships was well below the entry qualifications to coaching scheme C groups.
Others	Those having good hand–eye coordination, general athletic ability, basic skills in the sport, being good enough to represent their school (but not their district), having the potential to go on to greater things, and having a commitment to attend.

The children

Sport	Sex	Age group	Ability level
Cricket	Boys	13–14	Participation (top end)
Hockey	Mixed	12–13	Participation
Rugby union	Boys	12–13	Participation (top end)
Soccer	Mixed*	11–12	Participation (top end)
Swimming	Mixed	11–14	Participation
Tennis	Mixed	10–12	Participation

*Only boys responded, however.

The coaches

Sport	No. children in squad	Head coaches	Assistant coaches	Ratio of coaches:children
Cricket	30	1	3	1:7
Hockey	29	1	2	1:10
Rugby union	26	1	2	1:10
Soccer	30	1	2	1:10
Swimming	25	1	1	1:12
Tennis	24	1	2	1:8

The facilities

Sport	Facility	Owned by	Hourly hire rate
Cricket	Sports hall (leisure centre)	City of Bradford Recreation Division	Free
Hockey	Sports hall (activities centre)	City of Bradford Recreation Division	Free
Rugby union	Pitch (club)	Bradford and Bingley RUFC	£200 total
Soccer	Sports hall (activities centre)	City of Bradford Recreation Division	Free *
Swimming	Pool (dual use)	City of Bradford	Free*
Tennis	Sports hall (activities centre)	City of Bradford Recreation Division	Free

*Use of pool at time agreed by school.

How the scheme was managed

Major partner: City of Bradford Metropolitan Council Recreation Division
Project manager: Deiniol Williams

The Scheme Liaison Officer works for the Policy and Resources Officer, City of Bradford Metropolitan Council Recreation Division. *Time spent on project:* 10–12 hours per week.

Management structure

```
City of Bradford Metropolitan Council
            │
    Recreation Division
            │
   Six Schools of Sport
```

Other agencies involved

City of Bradford Youth and Community Education Services

About the coaches

Five of the assistant coaches were PE teachers; none of the head coaches were.

Payment per hour for assistant coaches: £7.50

Minimum qualifications for assistant coaches: lower levels of national governing body awards. Many were in fact more highly qualified.

Extra training provided: none, but only because the planned courses with the National Coaching Foundation were cancelled owing to shortage of time.

Transport

The transport was provided mainly by the parents and the schools. Costs incurred by the schools were reimbursed by the scheme. In some instances taxis were hired and day-rover bus passes provided.

Promoting the scheme

Letters, poster and leaflets were sent to schools. The value of after-school sport was discussed with headteachers and PE staff, and also in a a press article. Coaches were contacted by letter. Parents were informed of their child's selection with a letter via the children.

Publicity and promotion was not a big issue in Bradford, and recruiting the children was not a problem either.

Additional funding

Contribution from children: none

How the money was spent

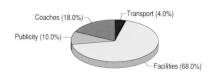

Coaches (18.0%) — Transport (4.0%)
Publicity (10.0%)
Facilities (68.0%)

Strengths of the scheme

● Good coaches, who are mostly Sports Development Officers.

● Use of facilities during off-peak periods kept down the cost.

● The project boosted resources that can be used again. The Sports Development Officers welcome this purchase of new equipment because it supports their work.

● The principle of the scheme was already accepted — the Recreation Division has credibility in providing opportunities for children after school.

● The way in which the project was 'sold' to schools by personal visits and discussions by Scheme Liaison Officer and head coaches. This built on the existing good relationship with schools.

● The Scheme Liaison Officer is at senior manager level in the Recreation Division and has close knowledge of the operational needs of the service and sports development issues.

Weaknesses

● The duration of the scheme was possibly too short.

● There were problems managing the project alongside current work.

● Uncertainty about the funding of Phase Two made it hard to plan for the future.

Competition

The tennis school of sport is to organise an inter-school short-tennis competition. Children from the rugby union school of sport played a series of matches against teams from other schemes.

New links

Headteachers and PE teachers have 'come out of the woodwork'! It remains to be seen whether links with clubs will be formed when the exit routes take shape. In cricket, contact has been wider than with just the clubs — major new links have been formed with the general cricketing population.

Scope for development

Discussions will be held with the Sports Development Officers at the end of the current scheme about how the exercise can be repeated at the beginning of 1992.

It must be pointed out (or confessed!) that there is excess funding available from the initial allocation. This will be used to extend the scheme. Additional resources from within the Sport and Young People Project will be used to boost this development. Soccer and swimming may be dropped in favour of badminton and netball.

Other comments

An important issue for us both before and during the scheme has been that funds available for transporting children, many of whom would not otherwise have chosen to attend at the various centres, has made a

considerable impact on participation.

However, the most important issue to arise from this project in Bradford is the readiness of school PE staff and head-teachers to respond in a very positive way to increased opportunities for their pupils to take part in after-school sporting activities that they themselves cannot provide.

Scheme

4

Bristol Champion Coaching

Scheme Liaison Officer: Dave Travis
Job title: Director of Coaching
Scheme address:
c/o Withywood School Campus
Molesworth Drive
Withywood
Bristol
BS13 9PL
Telephone: 0272 783141

The Schools of Sport

The Schools of Sport ran twice a week over a six-week period. All took place after school.

Children enrolled	218
Number of sessions	12
Potential attendances	2616
Actual attendances	1674
Percentage attendance	**64%**

Choosing the children

Sport	Selection criteria
All	Children from disadvantaged areas of Bristol who have good potential (i.e. good motor skills and physical aptitude), and who show a determination to continue with the chosen sport after the scheme, but excluding those already playing the sport competitively within a club.

Recruiting the children

Selected schools with children from the disadvantaged areas of Bristol were invited after discussion with headteachers and heads of PE. A meeting was then set up with every school to explain the ethos and criteria more fully. The teachers then selected children from their school in order of priority. The Scheme Liaison Officer made the final selections in order to juggle numbers between the schools and sports.

Bristol Champion Coaching was conceived at a meeting in May 1991 between the Project Coordinator and the South West Sports Council, where it was decided to target the disadvantaged city areas and the schools that serve them.

It was felt that the vital ingredient of a scheme of this type would be the contact with the participating schools and the subsequent recruitment, and so a steering group was formed, comprising the SLO, Sports Council and City Council representatives, and two heads of PE from target schools. This group remained a cornerstone of the scheme and helped greatly in keeping contact with participants over issues that inevitably arose.

The children

Sport	Sex	Age group	Ability level
Badminton	Mixed	13–14	
Basketball	Mixed	13–14	
Cricket	Mixed	13–14	
Hockey	Mixed	13–14	Recruited at performance level, but in
Netball	Girls	13–14	practice many were at participation level.
Rugby union	Boys	13–14	
Table tennis	Mixed	13–14	
Tennis	Mixed	13–14	

The coaches

Sport	No. children in squad	Head coaches	Assistant coaches	Ratio of coaches:children
Badminton	26	1	2	1:8
Basketball	30	1	4	1:6
Cricket	23	1	1	1:12
Hockey	31	1	4	1:6
Netball	30	1	4	1:6
Rugby union	30	1	3	1:7
Table tennis	21	1	3	1:5
Tennis	27	1	3	1:7

The facilities

Sport	Facility	Owned by	Hourly hire rate
Badminton	Sports hall (leisure centre)	Bristol City Council	£14.00
Basketball	Sports hall (school)	County of Avon	Free
Cricket	Sports hall (school)	County of Avon	Free
	Sports hall (leisure centre)	Bristol City Council	£47.00
Hockey	Pitch	Bristol Polytechnic	£23.00
Netball	Sports hall (leisure centre)	Bristol City Council	£14.00
Rugby union	Pitch (club)	Bristol RFC	£ 7.50
Table tennis	Sports hall (school)	County of Avon	Free
Tennis	Sports hall (school)	County of Avon	Free

How the scheme was managed

Major partner: Bristol City Council
Project manager: Dave Travis, Kate Falkner (Bristol City School Sport Liaison Officer).

The Scheme Liaison Officer is employed by Sun Life Sportschool. *Time spent on project:* difficult to quantify since it merged legitimately into my normal work, but it was considerable, and at its peak was mainly after normal hours. Any future scheme will require a full-time position.

Management structure

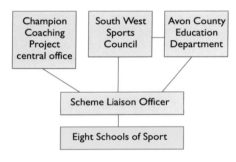

- Champion Coaching Project central office
- South West Sports Council
- Avon County Education Department
- Scheme Liaison Officer
- Eight Schools of Sport

About the coaches

Two head coaches and three assistant coaches were PE teachers.

Payment per hour for assistant coaches: £10.00

Minimum qualifications for assistant coaches: decided for each sport by head coaches, although the minimum national governing body qualification was the basic requirement.

Extra training provided: none

Transport

All the transport was provided by privately-hired buses, minibuses and taxis, paid for at commercial rates, and running on routes organised by the Scheme Liaison Officer. This expensive arrangement needed refining after initial problems, but held together and enabled all the participants to go virtually from door to door for six weeks.

Promoting the scheme

Letters were sent to headteachers and PE departments, posters and leaflets were distributed to schools, and announcements were made in assemblies. Parents were invited to the 'Young People in Sport' workshop.

Additional funding

Contribution from children: none

How the money was spent

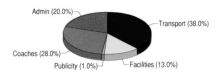

Admin (20.0%)
Transport (38.0%)
Coaches (28.0%)
Publicity (1.0%)
Facilities (13.0%)

Strengths of the scheme

- Established school links through Sun Life Sportschool and Bristol City Council created a good personal and working relationship.
- A good coach–pupil ratio meant quicker progress, and the payment created good will for the future.
- Transport network. This was the only way to guarantee attendance throughout the city.
- The large number of sports.
- The scheme provided the opportunity for disadvantaged areas that is not normally possible.
- Twice-weekly schools ensured a substantial amount of input per participant.

Weaknesses

- Short period of Schools of Sport. The enthusiasm of the children to continue could not be met, despite the exit routes.
- Difficulties with weather and light.
- Some coaches were not local, which made it difficult to plan exit routes and create local links.
- Planning time was too short.
- The Scheme Liaison Officer job was too demanding on top of the full-time job.
- The organisation was too big to control city-wide.
- There were problems with the transport network.
- The attendance rate was relatively low.

Competition

Some informal competition was included within the Schools of Sport.

New links

New links have been formed with schools, but they are specific to Dave Travis and Kate Faulkner, rather than ones which will be useful to Champion Coaching in the future.
    Contact with local clubs was not as effective as it could or should have been —

some head coaches were not local to Bristol. Links with clubs may be made in time, by they were not obvious during the scheme.

Scope for development

In the short term, an underspend means that some of the Schools of Sport will be kept going for a short period.
    In the long term, if the scheme is repeated in any form, it will make more sense to base the coaching in the schools, saving on the costs and headaches of transport. The money saved could pay for more coaches over a much longer time period. There are facility implications to this, but it would give a much better chance of consolidating real change in the local communities through the schools.

Other comments

I am not convinced that the expenditure on the administration and promotional side (*SportLogs*, Parent Packs, T-shirts, posters, etc.) was necessary. There was no evidence that it made much practical difference to the participants. The money would have been better spent on paying coaches to continue their Schools of Sport over a much longer period. The project has created a new appetite and demand — can this be met by existing structures?

Scheme

5

Bromley Champion Coaching

Scheme Liaison Officer: Ms Bernie Hamill
Job title: Sports Development Officer
Scheme address:
Leisure Services Department
Central Library
High Street
Bromley
BR1 1EX
Telephone: 081-464 3333 ext. 3510

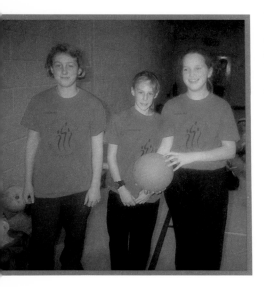

The London Borough of Bromley's Sports Development Team were able to take on the Champion Coaching Project and include it as part of their overall work programme. The existing infrastructure in terms of good communication with other agencies, and close cooperation with teachers, coaches, clubs and parents, enabled the team to devise effective exit routes for the six chosen sports. Examples of our existing schemes are the Bromley Cricket Partnership, the Bromley Borough Hockey Development Scheme, and the Crystal Palace Football in the Community scheme. In addition, players from tennis, basketball and netball are being fed into existing clubs.

The Schools of Sport

The Schools of Sport ran once a week for six weeks (seven weeks for tennis). Most took place after school, although there were two evening and two weekend sessions.

Children enrolled	414
Number of sessions	6
Potential attendances	2484
Actual attendances	1869
Percentage attendance	**75%**

Recruiting the children

All children, except those in the hockey group, were nominated by their PE teachers, who had met with the Scheme Liaison Officer beforehand to discuss the criteria for selection. For hockey, a trial, to which all schools were invited to send team players, was organised by the head coach.

Choosing the children

Sport	Selection criteria
Basketball	Team members showing the right commitment, aptitude, skill level and behaviour both on- and off-court.
Cricket	For boys, proven ability at school-team level. For girls, interest in the game and good hand-eye coordination skills.
Hockey	Skills trial by head coach.
Netball	School-team players.
Soccer	For boys, those who do not currently represent school or club, but who are potentially interested. For girls, those who have specified an interest and who are prepared to commit themselves to the scheme.
Tennis	School-team players, but excluding those who also play at county or club match level.

How the scheme was managed

Major partner: London Borough of Bromley Leisure Services Department
Project managers: Leisure Services and Education representatives

The Scheme Liaison Officer is employed by the London Borough of Bromley Leisure Services Department. *Time spent on project:* difficult to quantify since the hours per week varied both during the setting-up stage and the weeks of the scheme itself, but 10 hours per week would be close. Delegation was the key to reducing the hours.

Management structure

Other agencies involved

London Borough of Bromley Hockey Development Scheme
Crystal Palace Football Club Football in the Community
Association of Kent Cricket Clubs

About the coaches

Nine assistant coaches were PE teachers; no head coaches were.

Payment per hour for assistant coaches: £10.70

Minimum qualifications for assistant coaches: PE teachers or relevant coaching qualification as set out in national governing body coach profile form initially given out.

Extra training provided: assistant coaches were given the chance of attending National Coaching Foundation courses operating at the Crystal Palace National Sports Centre.

Transport

Transport was provided by PE teachers in local-school transport. Additionally, a minibus was hired to take two groups of basketball players from two schools to the Crystal Palace National Sports Centre for the six weeks of the scheme.

Promoting the scheme

The scheme was publicised with posters, press releases in local papers and via PE staff in schools. Details of the scheme were included in our Sports Development Newsletter, which is distributed to schools and sports clubs. Coaches were contacted via the head coach and through the publicity leaflet.

Once the children were selected, letters were sent to the parents explaining the philosophy behind the project. The parents were also invited to a 'Young People in Sport' workshop.

The cooperating agencies were sent posters and background material and were then seen personally by the Sports Development Officers.

Problems with other agencies

There seemed to be some conflict with some governing bodies as to the ability level at which the scheme was aimed.

Additional funding

Contribution from children: none

How the money was spent

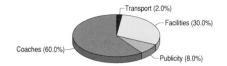

Transport (2.0%) — Facilities (30.0%) — Coaches (60.0%) — Publicity (8.0%)

Administration/office time was accounted for within the London Borough of Bromley's Sports Development budget.

Competition

No element of competition was included in the scheme.

Strengths of the scheme

● We already had a Sports Development Team with officers having a responsibility to develop particular sports (including four of the six in the scheme) in the community.

● An established communication network covering schools and clubs helped in the selection of the children and means that exit routes can be set up effectively.

● High-quality facilities.

Weaknesses

● There was not enough time for sufficient liaison with all the agencies. This stage is crucial for the coordination of the scheme. Also, October was the wrong time of year for some of the sports. However, the Sports Development Team enabled us to overcome some of these problems.

● We could only provide transport for a small group in one sport. Some children missed out because they could not travel across Bromley, which is the largest London borough.

● More *SportLogs* and T-shirts were needed.

New links

Fortunately, good links with schools already existed. Some clubs have seen the value of a

coordinated approach, combining valuable resources and channelling talent through to clubs. We have only touched the surface of parental involvement. We need to feed information to them and take their suggestions into account (we have given out our own 'talk back' forms for this).

Scope for development

Now that the scheme is up and running, we need to develop it into a year-round rolling programme, so that parents, clubs, coaches and teachers can access a particular sport at any given time. Furthermore, the quality of coaching can be improved by having a coach education strategy within the borough.

The impact of Champion Coaching across the borough has enabled a wide group of young people to develop their sporting potential after school and with continued support the scheme can go from strength to strength.

The children

Sport	Sex	Age group	Ability level
Basketball	Boys	12–14	Performance/excellence
Cricket	Girls	11–14	Participation
	Boys	11–14	Performance
Hockey	Girls/mixed	12–14	Performance
Netball	Girls	13–14	Performance
Soccer	Girls	11–12	Foundation
	Boys	13–14	Participation
Tennis	Girls/boys	12–13	Performance

The coaches

Sport	No. children in squad	Head coaches	Assistant coaches	Ratio of coaches:children
Basketball	37 + 20	1	4	1:8
Cricket	38 + 36	1	4	1:10
Hockey	22 + 38	1	4	1:12
Netball	23 + 30	1	3	1:13
Soccer	23 + 38 + 13	1	2	1:9
Tennis	4 × 24	1	1	1:12

The facilities

Sport	Facility	Owned by	Hourly hire rate
Basketball	Sports hall (school)	London Borough of Bromley	Free
	Arena	Crystal Palace NSC	£22.50
Cricket	Indoor cricket school	Howden Tennis Centre	£0.50 per child
	Sports hall (leisure centre)	London Borough of Bromley	Free
Hockey	All-weather pitch	Crystal Palace NSC	£41.00
	All-weather pitch	London Borough of Bromley	£12.00
Netball	Sports hall (school)	London Borough of Bromley	Free
	Sports hall (leisure centre)	London Borough of Bromley	£10.35
Soccer	Sports halls (school)	London Borough of Bromley	Free
Tennis	Indoor courts (club)	Bromley Lawn Tennis Club	£14.00 (2 cts)
	Courts (leisure centre)	London Borough of Bromley	Free
	Courts (club)	Bromley Lawn Tennis Club	Free

Scheme

6

Champion Coaching with the Sports Training Scheme (Nottinghamshire)

Scheme Liaison Officesr: Steve Grainger/Sue Conner
Job titles: Principal Officer (Sport) /Coordinator (Nottinghamshire Champion Coaching)
Scheme address:
Nottinghamshire Sports Coaching Centre
Sycamore Complex
Hungerhill Road
St Anns
Nottingham NG3 4NB
Telephone: 0602 624040

Because of the geographical size of Nottinghamshire it was decided to run Schools for each sport in each of its eight districts. Youngsters would then be selected, on the basis of potential and commitment, for the County School of Development, to run from January to March 1992. This approach meant that more than a thousand youngsters and ninety coaches were able to become involved in the scheme. Those participants not selected for the County Schools are to be catered for by follow-on Schools and by the creation of start-up grants. These grants, open to all facilities and coaches who had an involvement in the project, offer financial support to new junior sports clubs.

The Schools of Sport

Schools of sport ran in all eight districts of the county (there were forty-five schools in total). Phase One ran once a week for six weeks, after school. Phase Two will run for ten weeks.

Children enrolled	872
Number of sessions	6
Potential attendances	5232
Actual attendances	4447
Percentage attendance	**85%**

Recruiting the children

All the schools in the county were invited to send able players to district trials, at which the two coaches for each district school of sport selected children based on the criteria below.

At the end of Phase One, all districts will take part in a tournament, at which one county squad will be selected for Phase Two.

Choosing the children

Sport	Selection criteria
All	Able, but not county-level, players who had potential, were already aware of the basic skills of the game and could apply themselves to regular and intensive training.

How the scheme was managed

Major partner: Nottinghamshire County Council Leisure Services
Project managers: Sue Conner (project coordinator) through line management to Steve Grainger (Principal Officer (Sport)).

The Scheme Liaison Officers are employed by Nottinghamshire County Council Leisure Services. *Time spent on project:* Sue Conner: 12 hrs/week; Steve Grainger 2 hrs/week.

Other agencies involved

General Inspector for Physical Education

Management structure

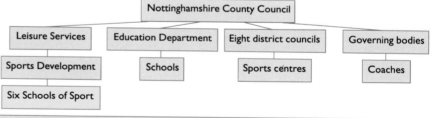

The children

Sport	Sex	Age group	Ability level
Basketball	Mixed	11–14	Mixed from foundation to performance
Hockey	Mixed	11–14	Mixed from foundation to performance
Netball	Girls	11–14	Mixed ability (mostly participation)
Rugby union	Boys	11–13	Mostly participation/performance
Soccer	Girls	11–14	Foundation/participation
Tennis	Mixed	11–14	Participation (top end)

The coaches

Sport	No. children in squad	Head coaches	Assistant coaches	Ratio of coaches:children
Basketball	24	1	1	1:12
Hockey	24	1	1	1:12
Netball	20	1	2	1:7
Rugby union	20	1	1	1:10
Soccer	16	1	1	1:8
Tennis	12	1	1	1:6

About the coaches

Thirty-three head and twenty-four assistant coaches were PE teachers.

Payment to coaches: for six-week course, trial and competition: head coach: £75; Assistant coach: £50.

Minimum qualifications for coaches:
Head coach: qualified to minimum governing body standards or qualified PE teacher with coaching experience in the sport.
Assistant coach: experienced in the sport with aspirations to coach (the idea is to increase the number of coaches in the county).

Extra training provided: briefing sessions for each sport led by the head coach.

Promoting the scheme

The scheme was publicised to children via posters in schools and recreation centres. PE teachers were written to and then contacted verbally. Sports clubs were contacted individually where appropriate, but the main thrust of the scheme was to improve school links. Coaches were recruited via national governing bodies and schools' associations. Parents were written to following their child's selection and invited to attend the final tournament.

Additional funding

Nottinghamshire County Council Leisure Services: £750 (administration support)
Revenue grant from East Midlands Sports Council: £8000
Nottinghamshire County Council Leisure Services: £4000
(both to continue the scheme in January to April)

Contribution from children: none

How the money was spent

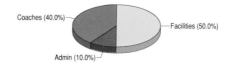

Coaches (40.0%) — Facilities (50.0%) — Admin (10.0%)

Strengths of the scheme

● Existing infrastructure developed over the last two and a half years through the Nottinghamshire Sports Training Scheme and the positive support of the County Council.

● The extra ten-week course maintained the children's interest and gave them a goal for which to aim.

● Participants had an introduction to the Schools of Sport within easy access of their home/school and as a result of this had more incentive to travel to the County School (in some cases this amounts to a ninety-mile round trip).

● Employing a part-time scheme co-ordinator who is a part-time teacher and who can relate to the circumstances of schools and PE teachers.

● Offering schools equipment vouchers in return for the use of their facilities.

Weaknesses

● There was a lack of time and resources for promotion and publicity, but having said that, few of the schools could have taken more.

● Lack of real understanding of the scheme by assistant coaches. There was a lack of resources with which to train assistant coaches. They would undoubtedly be more prepared to attend the briefing sessions now that they have seen the scheme in action.

Transport

Parents were asked to provide all transport.

Competition

Tournaments will be held at the end of Phase One.

New links

Many links have been created with schools since over half of the coaches were teachers and most of the facilities were school-based.

The scheme will hopefully produce new sports clubs. With equal funding from the East Midlands Sports Council and Nottinghamshire County Council, a 'start-up grant' scheme has been established to assist new clubs developing from the Champion Coaching scheme or the Nottinghamshire Sports Training Scheme.

Problems with other agencies

A few PE staff in the county felt the scheme was a threat to their extra-curricular activities and were therefore not prepared to lend their support.

Scope for development

Expansion of the scheme would require more emphasis on publicity at local level (funds would have to be provided for this). End-of-course tournaments could be arranged (again funds would be required). It would be better to run two follow-on courses, one in the north of the county and one in the south, rather than just the one planned.

The Champion Coaching scheme has captured the enthusiasm of coaches, children and parents alike, and has succeeded where other schemes have failed. It must at all costs be continued.

The facilities

A large number of facilities were used. Use of the majority was exchanged for equipment vouchers. Only those actually paid for are given below.

Sport	Type of facility	Owned by	Hourly rate
Basketball	Sports hall (dual use)	Mansfield DC/Nottinghamshire CC	£13.00*
	Sports hall (dual use)	Bassetlaw DC/Nottinghamshire CC	£30.98*
Hockey	Pitch (leisure centre)	Mansfield District Council	£24.00 session
	Pitch (leisure centre)	Bassetlaw District Council	£141.05 total
Netball	Sports hall (youth centre)	Broxtowe District Council	£150.00 total
	Sports hall (leisure centre)	Bassetlaw District Council	£137.10 total
Rugby union	Pitch (club)	Mellish RUFC	£75.00 total*
Soccer	Pitch (leisure centre)	Broxtowe District Council	£21.00 session
	Pitch (leisure centre)	Mansfield District Council	£11.20 session
	Pitch (park)	Ashfield District Council	£15.00 session
Tennis	Courts (leisure centre)	Newark and Sherwood District C	£112.00 total
	Courts (leisure centre)	Mansfield District Council	£ 0.60 per crt
	Courts (leisure centre)	Bassetlaw District Council	£15.90 session
	Courts (leisure centre)	Ashfield District Council	£ 5.50 per crt

* Plus equipment voucher

Scheme

7

Chelmsford Champion Coaching

Scheme Liaison Officer: Jon Roberts
Job title: Sports Link Coordinator
Scheme address:
Chelmsford Borough Council Leisure
    Services
Duke Street
Chelmsford
CM1 1JE
Telephone: 0245 490490 ext. 3318

Who, six months ago, would have thought that Chelmsford Champion Coaching would have been possible? This is an achievement based on highly successful partnerships with local authorities, schools, regional and county governing bodies and local sports clubs. The whole initiative was developed in six months — what could we achieve over two years?

We were pleased to be associated with Essex County Cricket Club, who hosted our cricket School of Sport, at which the coach was county wicketkeeper Mike Garnham. As a result, three students have been selected for junior trial at the club — perhaps the scheme may have identified a future champion.

The Schools of Sport

The Schools of Sport ran once a week over a six-week period. Most took place in the early evening, but there were two after school and one at the weekend.

Children enrolled	157
Number of sessions	6
Potential attendances	942
Actual attendances	822
Percentage attendance	**87%**

Recruiting the children

All secondary schools in Chelmsford were invited to nominate in priority order five children for each sport, based on the criteria below (decided upon by the Scheme Liaison Officer and a senior PE teacher in the borough). Selection was then based on the availability of places on each school of sport and responses from the schools.

Choosing the children

Sport	Selection criteria
All	Children aged 11–14 (but not including the new intake) at the foundation, participation and performance levels, having an interest in sport, a positive attitude, and the basic skills required to participate effectively (for example, can bowl overarm in cricket). Excluding any child already being coached at school or club, or who is a member of a representative squad at district or county level.

How the scheme was managed

Major partner: Chelmsford Borough Council
Project manager: Jon Roberts

The Scheme Liaison Officer is employed by Chelmsford Borough Council, but part funded by the Sports Council. *Time spent on project:* a total of 25 hours during the planning stage and 45 hours during the delivery stage.

Management structure

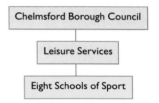

Other agencies involved

Chelmsford Women's Football Club

About the coaches

One head and three assistant coaches were PE teachers.

Payment per hour for assistant coaches: £10.00

Minimum qualifications for assistant coaches: intermediate coaching qualification with experience of working with children, or PE teacher with interest in the relevant sport.

Extra training provided: none

The children

Sport	Sex	Age group	Ability level
Basketball	Mixed	12–14	Foundation/participation
Cricket	Boys	12–14	Performance/excellence
Hockey	Mixed	12–14	Performance
Soccer	Girls	12–14	Foundation/participation
	Boys	12–14	Performance
Swimming	Mixed	12–14	Performance
Table tennis	Mixed	12–14	Foundation/participation
Tennis	Mixed	12–14	Performance

Transport

Transport was provided to venues by Champion Coaching itself or by a private company for all children on those Schools of Sport which began at 4pm, and between two main locations in the borough for all the weekday sports. One school is 17 miles from Chelmsford; to allow for its inclusion in the scheme, transport was provided to and from Chelmsford.

Promoting the scheme

Publicity to schools was through the PE Adviser and the Mid-Essex Secondary Schools Sports Association. PE teachers informed the children. There were also personal visits to schools by the Scheme Liaison Officer. The scheme was promoted generally in the local media, and officials of interested clubs were written to. All coaches were personally approached through regional governing bodies. Parents were written to after the selection of their child.

Additional funding

Contribution from children: none

How the money was spent

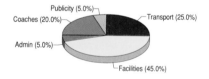

Publicity (5.0%)
Coaches (20.0%)
Transport (25.0%)
Admin (5.0%)
Facilities (45.0%)

Strengths of the scheme

● The support and help of a senior and highly respected PE teacher in the planning stage aided the design of the scheme.

● The high quality of the coaching provided an excellent scheme that was very much appreciated by parents and children alike.

● The use of school facilities has improved links with local clubs and opened many doors for future development. It also helped to keep costs down.

Weaknesses

● We encountered major logistical problems due to the size of the borough and the number of schools involved. The financial cost was considerable.

● The PE profession found it difficult to identify children in those sports not taught at their school.

Competition

The only competition was within each school of sport.

New links

A number of important new links have been created with schools, particularly those providing facilities. It is vital that these opportunities are developed so that the doors opened by Champion Coaching should not close again. Local clubs are very interested in extending their involvement in Champion Coaching and are keen to provide exit routes.

Scope for development

A future project would be best targeted at the needs of each sport in the area, and where possible linked to local clubs' coaching programmes to ensure exit routes for children and coaches.

The level of coaching was a major strength of the scheme, but employing coaches who were available after school proved difficult, since many work in London. A major component of future projects would have to be coach education support for club coaches, to ensure that the exit routes are into quality coaching.

Liaison with local schools must be improved to allow for greater coordination and reduced duplication of programmes.

The success of Champion Coaching has been significant, although a great deal of work is required to maintain the forward momentum. Chelmsford Sportslink, the

borough's programme to promote sporting opportunities for school-age children will continue to work for the increased coordination and cooperation that, as was shown by Champion Coaching, is essential in sports development. The intention is that the Champion Coaching Project concept will become an integral part of the Sportslink campaign.

Other comments

Future projects in Chelmsford would not be able to provide free transport because of financial restrictions — a charge to the participants would have to be made.

The coaches

Sport	No. children in squad	Head coaches	Assistant coaches	Ratio of coaches:children
Basketball	24	1	1	1:12
Cricket	18	1	2	1:6
Hockey	32	1	1	1:16
Soccer	20 + 20	1	1	1:10
Swimming	15	1	2	1:5
Table tennis	14	1	1	1:7
Tennis	14	1	1	1:7

The facilities

Sport	Facility	Owned by	Hourly hire rate
Basketball	Sports hall (school)	Essex County Council	£10.00
Cricket	Indoor nets (club)	Essex County Cricket Club	£400 total
Hockey	Artificial pitch	Chelmsford Borough Council	£32.50
Soccer	Artificial pitch	Chelmsford Borough Council	£32.50
	Artificial pitch (dual use)	Essex CC/Chelmsford BC	£10.00
Swimming	Pool (school)	Essex County Council	*
Table tennis	Gymnasium (school)	Essex County Council	£ 7.50
Tennis	Floodlit courts	Essex County Council	*

*Equipment grant used as payment.

Scheme

8

Cheshire Champion Coaching

Scheme Liaison Officer: Ken Williams
Job title: Project/Development Officer,
Cheshire County Council
Scheme address:
Fountains Building
Upper Northgate Street
Chester
CH1 4EF
Telephone: 0244 381931

The Cheshire Champion Coaching scheme was warmly welcomed by all the agencies participating. The young people, their parents and the coaches have all expressed the view that the benefits provided by this initiative ought to be available everywhere, over a wide range of sports, and on a regular basis. We managed to maintain a high ratio of coaches to children, which permitted a significant element of individual tuition. The scheme has contributed to the establishment of an equipment resource which will be used to expand sports development work in all parts of the county.

The Schools of Sport

The Schools of Sport ran for the five days (three days for rugby union) of the half-term holiday. They all took place during the daytime. The boys' soccer school was reserved for pupils with learning difficulties attending mainstream schools.

Children enrolled	140
Number of sessions	3, 5
Potential attendances	644
Actual attendances	622
Percentage attendance	**97%**

Recruiting the children

Three sports were promoted in each of the two district authorities involved. Twenty schools and two sports clubs nominated up to six children in order of preference in each sport, based on the criteria listed below. The head coach in each sport made the final selection, based on the recommendations of the schools and clubs, sometimes contacting the heads of PE departments for further advice and information.

Choosing the children

Sport	Selection criteria
Soccer (boys)	Pupils with learning difficulties attending mainstream schools.
All others	Those with a high level of natural sporting ability, with sufficient personal fitness to benefit from the concentrated contact time, with a positive attitude to learning, who are able and willing to attend all sessions, and who are likely to receive good family support.

How the scheme was managed

Major partner: Cheshire County Council
Project managers: Heritage and Recreation Service

The Scheme Liaison Officer is employed by Cheshire County Council. *Time spent on project:* 15 hours per week for 10 weeks.

Management structure

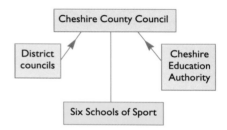

Other agencies involved

Cheshire County Education Authority
PE Advisory Staff, Cheshire County Council

About the coaches

Two head and five assistant coaches were PE teachers.

Payment per hour for assistant coaches: £10.00

Minimum qualifications for assistant coaches: national governing body basic/preliminary award.

Extra training provided: none, except that head coaches briefed the assistant coaches.

Transport

Parents assisted with transport.

The children			
Sport	Sex	Age group	Ability level
Cricket	Boys	11–14	Performance
Hockey	Mixed	11–14	Performance
Netball	Girls	11–14	Performance
Rugby union	Boys	11–14	Performance
Soccer	Girls	11–14	Participation
	Boys	11–14	Participation

Promoting the scheme

Because we joined the project later than most schemes, we concentrated our publicity directly at schools and two sports clubs. The scheme was also publicised via a press release and in a video made as it happened.

Additional funding

Contribution from children: none

How the money was spent

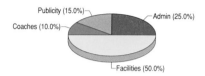

Strengths of the scheme

- The appointment of permanent Sports Development Officers, and excellent cooperation and liaison with education advisers and heads of PE departments, meant that high-quality, well-motivated coaches could easily be found.
- Wide use was made of the thirty-four joint-use sports centres in Cheshire, which offer excellent facilities.
- Equipment provision — sound financial budget.
- Dedicated management with established objectives.

Competition

Competitions between small groups or teams were included to provide a fun element and as a means of self-improvement skill testing and monitoring.

Weaknesses

- A lack of preparation time due to lateness in joining the scheme. Liaison and contact time was restricted to that after the summer vacation.
- We had some difficulty in appointing head coaches.
- A lack of transport restricted the operation of some Schools of Sport.
- A substantial amount of administration time was required by the Scheme Liaison Officer and the head coaches.

New links

The scheme has strengthened links with sports clubs, but not in all sports as yet, and with schools, in particular with heads of PE departments. We have also identified high-calibre coaches for future courses.

Scope for development

The scheme was restricted to two out of the eight district council authorities; the others could be targeted in the future. Also, other sports could be included in the scheme. Six to ten sports promoted throughout the eight districts could involve over two thousand children (the Cheshire Football Development Scheme recorded over thirty-three thousand attendances during 1990). Additional courses are already scheduled for 1992.

We would target children in the foundation and participation groups, who form the base of the pyramid. This work is currently in hand and is being undertaken by the Sports Development Officers. We would wish to appoint further Development Officers in other sports. Our objective is to work with the governing bodies of sport, sports clubs, school sports associations and PE advisory staff. Alongside this development we would continue to operate our Coach Education Programme, which is committed to producing two hundred new coaches every year.

Other comments

Champion Coaching has highlighted the opportunity to develop a national strategy, involving all those organisations concerned with the coaching of young people. Many questions are being asked and hopefully answered in a positive and challenging way. The benefits are enormous, not only to the young individuals willing to take up the challenge, but the impact this would engender to a future nation.

The coaches

Sport	No. children in squad	Head coaches	Assistant coaches	Ratio of coaches:children
Cricket	24	1	4	1:5
Football	16 + 16	1	1	1:8
Hockey	28	1	3	1:7
Netball	28	1	2	1:9
Rugby union	28	1	2	1:9

The facilities used

Sport	Facility	Owned by	Hourly hire rate
Cricket	Sports hall	All dual-use sports centres:	£20.00
Hockey	Artificial pitch	Cheshire Education Authority/	£24.00
Netball	Sports hall	local authority	£20.00
Rugby union	Pitch		£13.50
Soccer	Sports hall		£20.00
	Pitch		£13.50

Scheme

9

Coventry Champion Coaching

Scheme Liaison Officer: Andy Wright
Job title: Head of Sport and Recreation
Scheme address:
President Kennedy School and Community
College
Rookery Lane
Coventry
CV6 4GL
Telephone:
0203 637361 (Champion Coaching office)
0203 661416 (School)

The Coventry scheme aims to build upon the good practice that already exists in many sports in linking school and community. It has attempted to consolidate bridges between PE teachers, national governing bodies and local clubs in order that a more coordinated approach to coaching opportunities for pupils can be achieved. In aiming at those children who do not normally have access to a high level of coaching, the scheme has complemented and enhanced current provision. The Coventry scheme sees the role of the PE teacher as vital. They know their pupils' interests, abilities and sporting commitments, and have the experience and expertise to develop the scheme.

The Schools of Sport

The Schools of Sport ran once a week over a six-week period. They all took place after school.

Children enrolled	162
Number of sessions	6
Potential attendances	972
Actual attendances	900
Percentage attendance	**93%**

Recruiting the children

All children were nominated by their PE teachers. For cricket, hockey and rugby union there were two nominations (and two reserves) from each school. For basketball, netball and tennis there were five nominations per school, at least two of whom were selected after a trial at which attitude and enthusiasm were very important factors.

Choosing the children

Sport	Selection criteria
All	Those pupils who do not normally have access to a high level of coaching and who would commit themselves enthusiastically to a specialist coaching course.

How the scheme was managed

Major partner: Coventry City Council Education Authority
Project managers (Steering Group):
Mr B Laventure (PE Adviser),
Mr N Cowie (Sports Council),
Mr N Hammond (National Coaching Foundation),
Mr A Howitt (Leisure Services),
Mrs B Galsworthy (Head Coach — netball),
Mrs K Reynolds (PE teacher),
Mr A R Wright (Scheme Liaison Officer).

The Scheme Liaison Officer is employed by Coventry City Council Education Authority.
Time spent on project: 20 hours per week.

Management structure

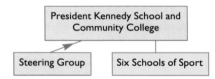

Other agencies involved

Warwickshire Rugby Football Union Development Scheme
Coventry and Warwickshire Basketball Development Scheme
Warwickshire Cricket Development Scheme

The children

Sport	Sex	Age group	Ability level
Basketball	Mixed	13–14	Participation/performance
Cricket	Boys	10	Participation/performance
Hockey	Mixed	13–14	Participation/performance
Netball	Girls	13–14	Participation/performance
Rugby union	Boys	13–14	Participation/performance
Tennis	Mixed	13–14	Participation/performance

The coaches

Sport	No. children in squad	Head coaches	Assistant coaches	Ratio of coaches:children
Basketball	28	1	2 (+1)*	1:7
Cricket	20	1	2	1:7
Hockey	30	1	2 (+1)*	1:7
Netball	30	1	2 (+1)*	1:7
Rugby union	30	1	2 (+1)*	1:7
Tennis	2 x 12	1	1	1:6

* These included 'guest' coaches, for example the England captain, international players.

About the coaches

Six assistant coaches were PE teachers; no head coaches were.

Payment for assistant coaches: each head coach was given £15 to pay assistants each week. If more was requested it was made available.

Minimum qualifications for assistant coaches: either to have the basic coaching award for the relevant sport, or to be a PE teacher, or to have proven ability/involvement with the sport.

Extra training provided: National Coaching Foundation courses were attended by some assistant coaches.

Promoting the scheme

PE teachers were sent publicity material for their school. All PE teachers and other interested persons were invited to a PE roadshow. Clubs were contacted via their head coach or by personal contact. Coaches were recruited directly by the Scheme Liaison Officer. Once the pupils had been nominated, their parents were invited to attend the 'Young People in Sport' evening.

The value of the scheme was publicised in the press and on local radio (CWR and Mercia), in the correspondence with PE teachers and headteachers (who were sent a parent pack), in a lecture to Sports Development students from Birmingham University and during consultations with the Coventry Schools Sports Federation.

Additional funding

West Midlands Sports Council: £3130

Contribution from children: none

How the money was spent

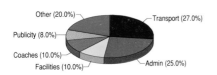

- Other (20.0%)
- Transport (27.0%)
- Publicity (8.0%)
- Coaches (10.0%)
- Facilities (10.0%)
- Admin (25.0%)

Other expenses: monitoring and evaluation; planning time (PE Teacher Development Group).

Transport

Although several parents helped as drivers, the scheme required extra transport in the form of school minibuses and taxis. Action Sport minibuses (run by Leisure Services) were also used.

Strengths of the scheme

- We complemented and supplemented the existing provision.
- Transport was provided and no charge was made, thus allowing any child to take part.
- The excellent qualifications, delivery and commitment of the coaches.
- A willing and able link person at each venue ensured that there were no problems with facilities or equipment.
- The support and assistance of the Steering Group and the PE Teachers Development Group.
- The personal relationship between the coaches and project coordinator, strong and enthusiastic links with the schools, the fact that we avoided clashes with established after-school clubs, and wide consultation all helped the scheme to run successfully.
- The willingness of the coaching staff to share ideas, expertise and methods with each other, across the range of sports.

Weaknesses

- Much emphasis has been put on getting a good head coach but nothing was done for assistants. *CoachLogs*, parent packs, sweatshirt should all have been supplied, and the views of the assistant coaches obtained.
- Everything was very rushed owing to the late appointment of the Scheme Liaison Officer. This meant that the PE profession did not become part of the planning process, and some were thereby alienated.
- The after-school period is the worst time to get transport. Local coach firms could not respond.

Competition

No element of competition was included.

New links

Coaches from many local clubs were used as assistants. This should prove beneficial for the future development of Champion Coaching.

Scope for development

PE teachers, including those who were not involved in this first phase, should be involved in a development group, where their views about the best way forward should be sought. The active support of headteachers should be gained.

There should be consultation with parents for ideas, observations and potential support (as coaches and drivers for

example), and with key local governing body personnel.

Assistant coaches should be assessed for their availability, willingness and qualifications to act as head coaches for the next phase. We should talk to the National Coaching Foundation contact about coach education and PE teachers and club players should be encouraged to gain coaching qualifications.

The high status of taking part in Champion Coaching has been established with the pupils, their parents and the teaching profession. It is hoped that these partnerships will develop in the future.

The facilities

Sport	Facility	Owned by	Hourly hire rate
Basketball	Sports hall (community schl)	Coventry Education Authority	*
Cricket	Sports hall (school)	Coventry Education Authority	£50 donation
Hockey	Astroturf pitch (school)	Bablake School (private)	£10 / session
Netball	Sports hall (community schl)	Coventry Education Authority	£100 donation
Rugby union	Gym/floodlit pitch (com. schl)	Coventry Education Authority	£100 donation
Tennis	Indoor courts (club)	Coventry Racket Centre	£ 4.50

*Equipment donation to the school.

Scheme
10

Derby Champion Coaching

Scheme Liaison Officer: Keith Twiss
Job title: Sports Development Officer
Scheme address:
The Council House
Corporation Street
Derby
DE1 2XJ
Telephone: 0332 255659

The Derby scheme was based on highly successful existing coaching projects implemented by the Sports Development Unit. This enabled the unit to build the additional Champion Coaching objectives into its overall framework. Local knowledge enabled the Sports Development Unit to advise on certain potential participants who we felt should be on the course, but who had slipped through their school's net. The fact that Mick Woolley was both a head coach and a member of the Sports Development Unit meant that a special insight could be gained into the strengths and weaknesses of the scheme.

The Schools of Sport

The Schools of Sport ran once a week over a six-week period. They all took place after school.

Children enrolled	120
Number of sessions	6
Potential attendances	720
Actual attendances	684
Percentage attendance	**95%**

Recruiting the children

A letter was sent to the head of PE at fourteen of the secondary schools in Derby requesting nominations for children to be included in the scheme. Details of four children for each sport, listed in priority order, were requested. Two places per school per sport were guaranteed, although the Sports Development Unit increased the quota where appropriate.

Choosing the children

Sport	Selection criteria
All	Those children representing their school and having the potential to make county or governing body squads (but not in them already), who would greatly be helped by the high-quality instruction that the scheme could provide. In addition, the children had to possess the necessary enthusiasm, attitude and commitment to their sport.

How the scheme was managed

Major partner: Derby City Council
Project managers: Sports Development Unit, Leisure Services Department.

The Scheme Liaison Officer is employed by Derby City Council Leisure Services Department. *Time spent on project:* 10 hours per week.

Management structure

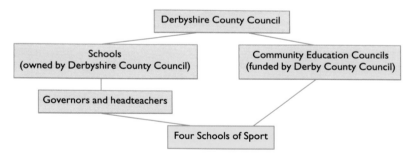

The children

Sport	Sex	Age group	Ability level
Basketball	Mixed	11–14	Participation/performance
Cricket	Mixed	11–14	Participation/performance
Netball	Girls	11–14	Participation/performance
Rugby union	Boys	13	Participation/performance

The coaches

Sport	No. children in squad	Head coaches	Assistant coaches	Ratio of coaches:children
Basketball	25	1	1	1:12
Cricket	28	1	3	1:7
Netball	33	1	2	1:11
Rugby union	28	1	1	1:14

About the coaches

One of the head and two of the assistant coaches were PE teachers.

Payment per hour for assistant coaches: £6.25

Minimum qualifications for assistant coaches: preliminary coaching award (Leader awards not sufficient).

Assistant coaches were specifically chosen on the basis of excellent work previously undertaken by the department and also because of their motivation and commitment to junior sport. Many of these should make first-class head coaches in the future.

Extra training provided: liaison meetings took place between the head coach and assistant coaches, where the philosophy and practical plan for the scheme were outlined.

Transport

Transport was arranged informally by the children and their parents.

Promoting the scheme

The heads of PE at the fourteen secondary schools who were to be part of the scheme were sent letters, publicity material and nomination forms. We relied on children seeing the posters and leaflets sent to the schools. We gave information leaflets directly to coaches whom we specifically wished to work on the scheme. The letters sent to the schools and information given to the press outlined fully the positive benefits of high-quality after-school sport.

Additional funding

Rugby Football Union: £70
    (10 rugby balls)
Nottingham, Lincolnshire and Derbyshire
    Rugby Football Union — Sir Anthony
    Walton Trust: sponsoring Derby District
    team to be formed from Champion
    Coaching squad: £100

Contribution from children: none

How the money was spent

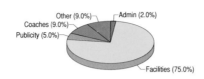

Other (9.0%) — Admin (2.0%)
Coaches (9.0%)
Publicity (5.0%)
Facilities (75.0%)

Other expenses: National Coaching Foundation courses and catering for 'Young People in Sport' workshop.

Competition

The basketball group played teams from Leicester and Thames Valley as the curtain-raisers to two Derbyshire v Buckinghamshire National League basketball games.

Strengths of the scheme

● The existing Sports Development Unit has broad experience of organising sports coaching courses across the city and also therefore a knowledge of the type of children who would profit from the scheme. In addition, we had the administrative infrastructure on hand to operate the project professionally.

● The head coaches and assistant coaches were top-quality people with a high degree of enthusiasm and commitment.

● The Sports Development Unit's existing links with secondary schools enabled us to use their high-quality facilities for the scheme.

● We adhered strictly to our specific criteria, and this produced the quality we sought.

● Pre-course meetings were held with coaches at which the aims, objectives and format which the Champion Coaching Project would take were discussed, thus ensuring consistency across the Schools of Sport.

● At each coaching session a member of the Sports Development Unit attended to monitor the session. This ensured that venues were available, caretakers present to open up, double bookings did not occur, all equipment was in place and that all administration was taken care of.

Weaknesses

● Interaction with PE teachers. Although many schools were visited by our unit's staff to explain the philosophy of the project and to seek teachers' support, there was simply not enough time to do this comprehensively.

● Interaction with PE advisers. This was mainly overlooked in the haste to produce the scheme.

● The time scale from the inception of the scheme to the actual Schools of Sport was totally unrealistic.

New links

The links with schools which had been made during other ventures by the department were strengthened by the scheme. A

stronger and firmer relationship has been forged with Derby Rugby Union Football Club, although some cooperation with the department had existed beforehand.

Scope for development

The scheme could be developed in a variety of ways. The numbers of children taking part in the existing sports could be increased by utilising other school facilities and other coaching talent. In addition, extra sports could be added to the four being promoted under the scheme. Greater parental involvement could be sought in administration and fund-raising.

The facilities

Sport	Facility	Owned by	Hourly hire rate
Basketball	Sports hall (community sch'l)	Derbyshire County Council	£30.00
Cricket	Sports hall (community sch'l)	Derbyshire County Council	£20.00
Netball	Sports hall (community sch'l)	Derbyshire County Council	£20.00
	Sports hall (community sch'l)	Derbyshire County Council	£20.00
Rugby union	Pitch (club)	Derby RUFC	£12.50

Scheme

11

Ealing Champion Coaching

Scheme Liaison Officer: Sam Robson
Job title: Sports Development Manager
Scheme address:
Leisure Services
Perceval House
14–16 Uxbridge Road
Ealing
London
W5 2HL
Telephone: 081-758 5210

The Schools of Sport

The Schools of Sport ran once a week over a six-week period. They all took place after school.

Children enrolled	240
Number of sessions	6
Potential attendances	1440
Actual attendances	1008
Percentage attendance	**70%**

Recruiting the children

Leaflets for each school of sport were distributed around the schools closest to the venue for that school of sport. Details were given in local papers, the Council's borough magazine and school assemblies. We held selection days for some sports; the others were open to all.

Choosing the children

Sport	Selection criteria
Basketball (boys)	Selection day based on age, skills and small group games.
Soccer (boys)	Selection day based on age, skills and small group games.
Netball	Selection day from school 1st team.
All others	These were fun coaching sessions — we took everyone who attended.

How the scheme was managed

Major partner: London Borough of Ealing
Project manager: Ealing Sports Development Scheme (four team members)

The Scheme Liaison Officer is employed by the London Borough of Ealing. Time spent on project: 4–5 hours per week.

Like many London boroughs, Ealing has a great variety of inhabitants, including traditionally well-off areas in the centre and a large Asian and Afro-Caribbean population. Our challenge was to provide sporting opportunities that would satisfy these diverse needs. The locations of the Schools of Sport were important — they were placed near willing sports clubs, but also near the centre of the catchment area. The boys' hockey sessions were held at the base of several Asian hockey clubs in the heart of Southall, a predominantly Asian area. In contrast, the girls' hockey was located close to Ealing Ladies Hockey Club, and attracted girls from the local private schools.

The children

Sport	Sex	Age group	Ability level
Basketball	Boys*	11–14	Participation/performance
	Girls	11–14	Participation
Hockey	Boys	11–14	Participation/performance
	Girls*	11–14	Performance
Netball	Girls	11–14	Performance
Soccer	Boys	11–14	Performance
	Girls*	11–14	Participation

*These were additional 'unofficial' Schools of Sport, run alongside the official schools because there was so much demand for places. Only the children on the official schemes received SportLogs, T-shirts, etc.

The facilities

Sport	Facility	Owned by	Hourly hire rate
Basketball	Sports hall (school)	London Borough of Ealing	£10.00
	Sports hall (leisure centre)	London Borough of Ealing	£10.00
Hockey	Artificial pitch (leisure cntr)	London Borough of Ealing	£10.00
	Pitch (club)	Barclays Bank	£20.00
Netball	Sports hall (school)	London Borough of Ealing	£20.00
Soccer	Pitch (school)	London Borough of Ealing	£10.00
	Pitch (club)	London Transport	£20.00

Management structure

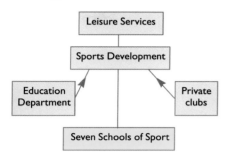

About the coaches

At the official Schools of Sport, three of the head and three of the assistant coaches were PE teachers. At the additional schools two of the head coaches and three of the assistants were.

Payment per hour for coaches: both head coaches and assistant coaches were paid £9.95 per hour, except for those who were already paid as part of the Sports Development Scheme.

Minimum qualifications for assistant coaches: experience in working with children in that sport.

Extra training provided: none, but we are building a coach development programme which will be offered free or at a reduced rate to coaches.

Promoting the scheme

Leaflets were distributed to PE teachers and children were told about the scheme in assemblies. Personal calls were also made to the schools. Clubs and coaches were contacted by telephone and later met personally. The scheme was featured in the local press, where the turn-up-and-take-part sessions were advertised. Parents were invited to attend the 'Young People in Sport' workshop.

Word of mouth was an extremely well-used vehicle of promotion, backed up by brightly coloured leaflets. All PE teachers in the thirteen high schools and several

private schools were visited and school assemblies taken in seven schools. The local papers supported the scheme well, providing regular updates and details of the turn-up-and-take-part schemes.

Transport

Special transport was required to take the netball players for their competition. Otherwise transport was arranged informally.

Additional funding

Ealing Borough Council Sports Development budget: £1458

Contribution from children: 50p per session, but this will go towards the child's membership of the appropriate sports club.

How the money was spent

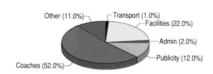

Other expenses: hockey qualification for the head coach; coach education (yet to be spent); additional T-shirts and prizes.

Strengths of the scheme

- There was a high black and Asian participation (greater than 50%) and a wide social-class range, reflecting the make up of the Borough.
- Hard work on good publicity and press coverage developed links with schools and the press.
- The assistance we got from the schools, PE teachers and the PE adviser, who are the best qualified and experienced in dealing with children.
- Links with local sports clubs.

Weaknesses

- The 'Young People in Sport' workshop was not a priority for parents and was not well attended.
- A lack of indoor venues.
- The scheme was biased towards the middle-class children.
- There was a lot of paperwork for the Scheme Liaison Officer and coaches.

Competition

Children from the netball school of sport played some matches against a team from the London Playing Fields Association scheme.

New links

There has been much more personal contact between the Sports Development team and both PE teachers and clubs. The scheme itself served as the catalyst.

Scope for development

The Sports Development team are keen to take on the idea of Champion Coaching to strengthen development in existing sports plus new areas, and also to involve different age groups (both younger and older).

The coaches

Sport	No. children in squad	Head coaches	Assistant coaches	Ratio of coaches:children
Basketball (boys)	40	1	3	1:10
(girls)	40*	1	2	1:13
Hockey (boys)	30*	1	3	1:7
(girls)	20*	1	3	1:5
Netball	60	1	3	1:15
Soccer (boys)	30	1	4	1:10
(girls)	20*	1	3	1:5

*Open sessions — turn up and take part.

Scheme

12

Hampshire Active Partners Champion Coaching

Scheme Liaison Officer: Steve Poynton
Job title: General Inspector: Physical
  Education
Scheme address:
Central Division Education Office
Southgate House
St Swithuns Street
Winchester
Hants
SO23 9EH
Telephone: 0962 869611

Hampshire has traditionally been supportive of after-school sport. However, the message of our own eyes and discussion linked to the debate on the National Curriculum PE proposals has led us to go into partnership with the Southern Region Sports Council to set up the Active Partners Project. This project aims to improve the quality of PE in Hampshire, to help pupils to participate both in and out of school, to develop partnerships and provide a structure for continuous and progressive sporting experience for children. Champion Coaching has added a further dimension and has given direction to aspects of the project's existing work.

The Schools of Sport

The Schools of Sport ran once a week for six to eight weeks. They took place when the facilities were available, two after school, three in the evening and one at the weekend.

Children enrolled	156
Number of sessions	6, 7, 8
Potential attendances	1014
Actual attendances	973
Percentage attendances	**96%**

Recruiting the children

The PE departments at all secondary schools were kept in touch with Active Partners, and later Champion Coaching. Areas for development and appropriate schools were identified. Information was sent to heads of PE and they informed and selected the pupils directly.

Choosing the children

Sport	Selection criteria
All	Those who are good all-round athletes or games players, have a strong interest in sport, are not currently receiving extensive coaching, are deserving of a reward, and are likely to want to continue the activity afterwards.

How the scheme was managed

Major partner: Hampshire LEA
Project managers: Principally the four PE Inspectors, although Active Partners has regular management meetings with the Southern Region Sports Council.

The Scheme Liaison Officer is employed by Hampshire County Council Education Department. *Time spent on project:* Difficult to quantify since the project is tied into Active Partners, which in turn is tied into support for schools.

The children

Sport	Sex	Age group	Ability level
Badminton	Boys/girls	11–14	Performance/excellence
Basketball	Boys/girls	11–14	Performance/excellence
Cricket	Boys	11–14	Performance/excellence
Hockey	Boys/girls	11–14	Performance/excellence
Netball	Girls	11–14	Performance/excellence
Tennis	Boys/girls	11–14	Performance/excellence

The coaches

Sport	No. children in squad	Head coaches	Assistant coaches	Ratio of coaches:children
Badminton	24	1	2	1:8
Basketball	30	1	5*	1:6
Cricket	24	1	2	1:8
Hockey	30	1	1	1:10
Netball	24	1	1	1:12
Tennis	24	1	2	1:8

*Advanced squad pupils.

The facilities

Sport	Facility	Owned by	Hourly hire rate
Badminton	Sports hall (leisure centre)	Portsmouth City Council	£21.50
Basketball	Sports hall (school)	Hampshire County Council	£15.50
Cricket	Sports hall (school)	Hampshire County Council	£ 4.70
Hockey	Fl'dlit all-weather pitch (club)	Trojans Club	£17.00
Netball	Sports hall (leisure centre)	Eastleigh Borough Council	£21.50
Tennis	Court (club)	Private	£20.00

Management structure

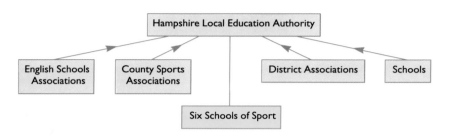

Hampshire Local Education Authority

English Schools Associations — County Sports Associations — District Associations — Schools

Six Schools of Sport

Other agencies involved

Active Partners Divisional Project Coordinators, schools, etc.

Transport

Where parents could not provide transport they were able to contact their child's school or the Scheme Liaison Officer. All bar one of these problems were sorted out at school level.

Promoting the scheme

Schools were contacted via PE Curriculum Support Groups; PE departments informed the children. Only clubs who could offer facilities were contacted at this stage. Once their child had been selected, parents were contacted by letter and invited to the 'Young People in Sport' workshop. The scheme was publicised in a press release via Hampshire County Council press office.

Additional funding

Administrators' time and costs from Active Partners budget: £1200

Contribution from children: none

How the money was spent

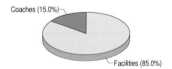

Coaches (15.0%)
Facilities (85.0%)

About the coaches

Five of the head coaches were qualified teachers or lecturers, four of them with PE-related qualifications. All the assistant coaches were PE teachers. However, a deliberate attempt was made, where possible, to involve potential future head coaches, good pupils, and coaches from those local clubs who were to provide the exit routes.

Payment per hour for assistant coaches: Valid expenses were paid at £10.00 per session (to avoid tax loss, etc.).

Minimum qualifications for assistant coaches: a variety of teaching/coaching qualifications, but more importantly, their quality as a person, i.e. known as a good coach/teacher; sensitive to youngsters' needs; motivated by the scheme.

Extra training provided: time restricted this to discusion with head coaches.

Strengths of the scheme

- The existence of Active Partners and that the scheme could be part of the infrastructure, and not 'bolt on'.
- The professionalism of the PE teachers over communication and selection.
- The professionalism of the head coaches and their perception of the project.
- Knowledge of the development needs of the sports concerned, gained through teachers, administrators from county sports associations, governing bodies and sports councils.
- Administrative backup in my own support section.
- Contact with the parents and the feedback they provided.

Weaknesses

- Communication. A full-time 'honest broker' is needed — busy people have to find time!
- This sort of scheme needs a support structure in place. Active Partners is 90 per cent there, but it is still early days really.
- Access to facilities.

Competition

Some Schools of Sport included a formal competitive element. Of these, some were structured on the internal programme and others involved local junior clubs, local schools district teams, etc.

New links

Existing school links have been complemented and clubs have been given access to to pupils. Links have also been formed with local authorities, leisure workers, school governors and parents.

Scope for development

Both Champion Coaching and Active Partners need a facilitator (or 'honest broker'); Active Partners is trying to establish this through Divisional Project Coordinators. This needs careful thought and attention.

All the interested groups need to formulate and agree an area-by-area development plan. Other agencies and sources of funding need to be drawn in.

It is hoped that most of the coaches will take part in Active Partners and the general

school-sport support offered. We need to develop a coach/teacher infrastructure, coach/teacher packs, agreed styles and formats for future schemes, coach/teacher refresher/induction courses, and work with PE Inspectors regarding direct school support. Liaison with the National Coaching Foundation's tutor in Hampshire has already begun.

Scheme

13

London Playing Fields Society — Champion Coaching

Scheme Liaison Officer: Alex Welsh
Job title: Centre Manager
Scheme address:
Douglas Eyre Sports Centre
Coppermill Lane
Walthamstow
London
E17 7HE
Telephone: 081-520 4918

The London Playing Fields Society, a registered charity, has a hundred-year history of providing playing opportunities for Londoners. In recent years, following Sports Council and Football Trust grants, the Society has established schemes which are continuous from school through to club level. Our role in Champion Coaching is as coordinator of those local agencies who have a vested interest in sports development. It attempts to help schools to extend and enrich their PE curricula in a way which makes maximum use of available resources, coaches and facilities, and thereby provides young people with the greatest opportunity for realising their potential.

The Schools of Sport

The Schools of Sport ran once a week over a six-week period. They all took place after school.

Children enrolled	262
Number of sessions	6
Potential attendances	1572
Actual attendances	1132
Percentage attendance	**72%**

Recruiting the children

Each school in Hackney and Waltham Forest was sent a form which outlined the philosophy of Champion Coaching and required them to nominate pupils in rank order for each school of sport. Teachers were asked to include information on pupils' experience and predicted progress. The Scheme Liaison Officer and the respective head coach selected pupils for the scheme. The selected children were notified personally. Parents were asked to give permission for their children to take part in the scheme.

Choosing the children

Sport	Selection criteria
All	Those demonstrating an innate or taught ability and a commitment to improving that ability.

How the scheme was managed

Major partners: London Boroughs of Hackney and Waltham Forest
Project manager: Alex Welsh

The Scheme Liaison Officer is employed by the London Playing Fields Society. *Time spent on project:* 10–12 hours per week.

Management structure

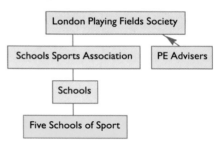

Other agencies involved

London Community Cricket Association

Transport

Transport was provided solely by parents and teachers.

The children

Sport	Sex	Age group	Ability level
Cricket	Mixed*	11–14	Performance/excellence
Hockey	Mixed	11–14	Performance/excellence
Netball	Girls	11–14	Performance/excellence
Soccer	Girls/boys	11–14	Performance
Tennis	Mixed	11–14	Performance/excellence

*Recruitment of girls was poor.

The coaches

Sport	No. children in squad	Head coaches	Assistant coaches	Ratio of coaches:children
Cricket	36	1	3	1:9
Hockey	69	1	3	1:16
Netball	30	1	2	1:17
Soccer	67	1	3	1:10
Tennis	60	1	2	1:20

About the coaches

One head and three assistant coaches were PE teachers. In addition, one of the head coaches was an ex-PE teacher.

Payment per hour for assistant coaches: £12

Minimum qualifications for assistant coaches: national governing body preliminary award.

Extra training provided: none, except for netball, where two of the assistant coaches qualified for a preliminary award as a result of taking part.

Promoting the scheme

Schools were circulated with information about the scheme, posters for display, etc. Information was also disseminated through PE advisers. Newspapers received press releases about the scheme. Local clubs (exit routes) were approached personally and where possible coaches were appointed from these clubs. The value of the scheme was stressed throughout.

Parents received information about the scheme when their children had been selected and were invited to attend the 'Young People in Sport' workshop.

Cooperating agencies were involved right from the outset so that they could make a valuable input to the shaping of the scheme.

Additional funding

Contribution from children: none

How the money was spent

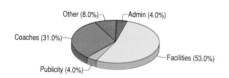

Other (8.0%), Admin (4.0%), Coaches (31.0%), Facilities (53.0%), Publicity (4.0%)

Other expenses: booking facilities for follow-up courses, fixtures, etc.

Competition

There was a competition element in the netball school of sport, who played against a team from the Ealing scheme.

Strengths of the scheme

● The Champion Coaching scheme was built on sound foundations already forged between the London Playing Fields Society and local schools.

● PE advisers from Hackney and Waltham Forest were totally supportive of the scheme.

● Links with local clubs led to accessible exit routes where pupils will experience further coaching and playing opportunities.

● The coaches are of such a high standard that the children have been highly motivated.

● High-quality facilities made coaching a pleasure.

Weaknesses

● Owing to the large catchment area it would have been impossible to transport all pupils to the various venues. We have all relied on parents and teachers to assist.

New links

The scheme has cemented the already sound links which had previously been established with schools. Our links with schools have always involved exit routes to

local clubs; the scheme has reinforced this.

The Champion Coaching Project has allowed the London Playing Fields Society virtually to organise district-based training (almost a mini system of centres of excellence).

Problems with other agencies

There was a lack of full cooperation from PE teachers. They should have been more involved with the scheme at the consultative stage. They feel that it has been imposed externally and therefore feel no sense of ownership. They are not all convinced of the benefits of Champion Coaching. Without full co-operation we risk alienating teachers and losing any support.

Scope for development

The London Playing Fields Society is already involved in activities involving primary schools, and an extension of Champion Coaching into this sector seems logical. Other local organisers of sports outside the London Playing Fields Society scheme have expressed a wish to be involved if the scheme expands. This would increase the number of Schools of Sport.

The facilities

Sport	Facility	Owned by	Hourly hire rate
Cricket	Sports hall (leisure centre)	London Borough of Waltham Forest	£15.80
Hockey	Floodlit artificial pitch	London Playing Fields Society	£25.00
Netball	Sports hall (leisure centre)	London Borough of Hackney	£20.00
Soccer	Floodlit artificial pitch	London Playing Fields Society	£25.00
Tennis	Indoor courts	Middlesex Polytechnic	£27.00

Scheme

14

Middlesbrough Champion Coaching

Scheme Liaison Officer: Ian Gardiner
Job title: Sports Officer
Scheme address:
Middlesbrough Leisure Services
Vancouver House
Gurney Street
Middlesbrough
TS1 1EL
Telephone: 0642 245432 ext. 3832

The Schools of Sport

The Schools of Sport ran once a week over a six-week period. They took place either after school or in the early evening.

Children enrolled	202
Number of sessions	6
Potential attendances	1212
Actual attendances	906
Percentage attendance	**80%**

Recruiting the children

The Scheme Liaison Officer contacted and met PE advisers, and subsequently met with soft-target schools. Nomination forms were then sent to schools. Children were then selected on a first-come-first-served basis. Those who could not be accommodated have been or will be found places on additional courses.

Choosing the children

Sport	Selection criteria
All	Players at foundation/ participation level who have not played for school, county or club teams, and who expressed a desire to join and attend the school of sport.

How the scheme was managed

Major partner: Middlesbrough Borough Council
Project managers: Ian Gardiner/ Middlesbrough Borough Council

The Scheme Liaison Officer is employed by Middlesbrough Leisure Services. *Time spent on project:* 8 hours per week (since 17 June 1991). An assistant has spent most of her working week on the project for 13 weeks.

Desmond Douglas — guest coach

When we were informed that we had been successful in securing Champion Coaching funding, we were clearly delighted!

Middlesbrough Champion Coaching was undoubtedly a success. We enrolled, coached and encouraged 183 children in seven sports, developed existing relationships with schools and teachers, and forged new links with coaches and voluntary clubs.

Sports development in Middlesbrough has benefitted enormously from our involvement in Champion Coaching. Phase Two will enable us to consolidate relationships further and will give more children the chance to participate.

The children

Sport	Sex	Age group	Ability level
Cricket	Mixed*	11–14	Foundation/participation
Hockey	Mixed	11–14	Foundation/participation
Netball	Mixed*	11–14	Foundation/participation
Rugby union	Mixed*	11–14	Foundation/participation
Soccer	Girls	11–14	Foundation/participation
Table tennis	Mixed	11–14	Foundation/participation
Tennis	Mixed	11–14	Foundation/participation

*There was only one girl on the rugby union course; there were no girls on the cricket course and no boys on the netball course.

The coaches

Sport	No. children in squad	Head coaches	Assistant coaches	Ratio of coaches:children
Cricket	28	1	2	1:9
Hockey	30	1	2	1:10
Netball	25	1	2	1:8
Rugby union	59	1	7	1:7
Soccer	22	1	2	1:7
Table tennis	20	1	2	1:7
Tennis	18	1	2	1:6

Management structure

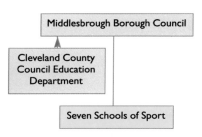

Other agencies involved

Cleveland County Council Education Department

About the coaches

One head and four assistant coaches were PE teachers.

Payment per hour for assistant coaches: £8.51

Minimum qualifications for assistant coaches: as specified by national governing bodies, but must express commitment to coaching, and particularly to coaching children.

Extra training provided: a special assistant coach training day was arranged, but sadly this had to be cancelled because the coaches had existing commitments to club sport.

Transport

Transport was arranged informally by children and parents.

Promoting the scheme

Schools were targeted individually after having been identified by the PE adviser. PE staff were then sent details of the scheme, together with publicity material, which was seen by the children. Visits were also made to schools. Press releases and adverts appeared in the local press.

Posters and leaflets were sent to local clubs and in some cases club contacts were used. Coaches were contacted through schools, clubs and via word of mouth.

Parents were invited to all six weeks of the scheme and to one sport-specific night, plus the 'Young People in Sport' workshop.

Additional funding

Middlesbrough Borough Council Leisure Services: £7160

Contribution from children: none

How the money was spent

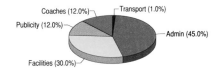

Strengths of the scheme

● Good organisation and administration avoided many problems.

● Publicity and promotion generated interest from fifty per cent more children than we could accommodate.

● High-quality coaches were obtained because of ongoing contact. They attended every session of every course.

● Our contingency planning helped when venues had to be re-arranged — for example, because of a waterlogged pitch.

● Excellent facilities.

● Parents, children and coaches were kept informed.

● Staff resources and sheer hard work and a commitment to sports development and the scheme.

● Existing contacts with clubs and schools.

Weaknesses

● Failure to capture the support of parents and PE staff.

● We decided initially that exit schemes would not be a main part of the scheme. We have largely stood by this, and have only become involved in exit schemes for rugby union and girls' soccer. We have, however, passed on a great deal of information to children (i.e. club contacts, coaches, venues, diet, exercises, etc.).

Competition

Competition was used only for children to be selected for a fair play award or as a representative for the School of Sport.

New links

Links with PE advisers, headteachers and PE staff have been strengthened. We now understand their problems better, which will serve us well as we approach Phase Two.

We have made particular strides with clubs that have hosted the schools of sport, although the contact with clubs with regard to exit schemes has been limited.

Problems with other agencies

There was dissatisfaction, disillusionment and lack of commitment to the scheme from PE advisers and staff in the schools.

Scope for development

Development will be through funding for Phase Two and the possible creation of a Sports Development Officer post for young people, through City Challenge central government funding.

The demand from children, the need to maintain links, and the amount we have learned and achieved means that there is a real need to expand the scheme beyond its now solid foundation, beyond a limited range of sports, and beyond soft-targeted schools.

Other comments

How long can local authorities continue to sustain quality coaching budgets? Should funding not be forthcoming from government, or from the National Coaching Foundation for that matter? Clearly, if local authorities are to continue without support. They may have to consider charging.

A large amount of money has been spent on the T-shirts, *SportLogs* and perks for the head coaches. I am worried that in subsequent schemes significant resources may be needed to meet the expectations created among children and coaches.

Assistant coaches should be provided with coach education, information packs, videos, equipment and clothing.

The facilities

Sport	Facility	Owned by	Hourly hire rate
Cricket	Sports hall (school)	Cleveland County Council	*
Hockey	Pitch (leisure centre)	Middlesbrough Borough Council	Free
Netball	Sports hall (school)	Cleveland County Council	*
Rugby union	Pitch (club)	Middlesbrough Rugby Club	£1000 total**
Soccer	Pitch (leisure centre)	Middlesbrough Borough Council	Free
Table tennis	Sports hall (leisure centre)	Middlesbrough Borough Council	Free
Tennis	Courts	Tennis World	£650 total†

*In exchange for equipment. **Including seven assistant coach fees.
†Including two assistant coach fees.

Scheme

15

Northamptonshire Champion Coaching

Scheme Liaison Officer: Adrian Lole
Job title: Principal Sports Officer
Scheme address:
Leisure Services
3rd Floor
Northampton House
Northampton
NN1 2HX
Telephone: 0604 237071

The overall theme for the Northamptonshire scheme is 'performance through partnership', reflecting the number of agencies involved in coordinating and delivering Champion Coaching.

As the scheme is a countywide initiative, centres were set up in five of the seven districts of Northampton-shire. For the centres, we selected two schools that were distinctly rural, while the others were in major towns. Five sports were chosen, with the aim of running every sport in every centre in Stage One. Stage Two will work on a one sport per centre basis, with head coaches selecting children for it from the first stage.

The Schools of Sport

The Stage One Schools of Sport ran once a week for a six-week period. Most took place after school or at the weekend; only two took place in the evening. Stage Two will also take place over six weeks.

Children enrolled	241
Number of sessions	6
Potential attendances	1446
Actual attendances	1100
Percentage attendance	**76%**

Recruiting the children

Initial recruitment took place at the schools where the activities were centred. Places were offered to feeder schools only if the main schools failed to recruit. Talks at school assemblies were followed by the distribution of application forms through heads of PE, who then helped in the selection of the pupils.

Choosing the children

Sport	Selection criteria
All (Stage One)	Those who are already playing the sport and are keen to learn and improve their standard, but excluding those already involved in high-level coaching in that sport.
All (Stage Two)	Those individuals showing the most commitment and improvement during Stage One, who are able to attend Stage Two.

About the coaches

Two head and five assistant coaches were PE teachers.

Payment for assistant coaches: £80 to cover the whole six weeks.

The head coaches were responsible for selecting and recruiting suitably qualified assistants.

Extra training provided: none so far, but there will be a programme of National Coaching Foundation courses to follow.

Transport

Transport was arranged informally by children, parents and schools.

Competition

Competition elements were left to the discretion of the head coaches.

How the scheme was managed

Major partner: Northamptonshire County Council Leisure Services
Project managers: Principal Sports Officer (Scheme Liaison Officer); School/Community Liaison Officer; Project Coordinator (Jon Ashby).

The Scheme Liaison Officer is employed by Northamptonshire County Council. The Project Coordinator was employed for 22.5 hours per week.

Management structure

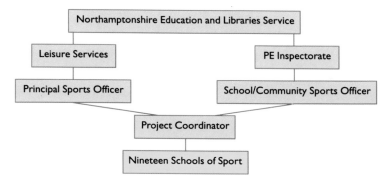

Promoting the scheme

The scheme was advertised in assemblies, school newspapers and via heads of PE. A press release was given to local newspapers.

Personal contact was made with clubs surrounding the targeted schools. Head coaches were given the responsibility of finding suitably qualified assistants.

Parents were told about the scheme via a handout given to children at the targeted schools, and were invited to attend the 'Young People in Sport' workshop.

Additional funding

East Midlands Sports Council: £3180

Contribution from children: £3.00 for the whole programme.

How the money was spent

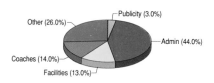

Other (26.0%)
Publicity (3.0%)
Admin (44.0%)
Coaches (14.0%)
Facilities (13.0%)

Other expenses: Stage Two and coach education.

Strengths of the scheme

● The spread around the county meant that a large number of schools were able to take advantage of the scheme.

● The two-stage approach provides a structured selection procedure in which the better or more committed students go on to Stage Two.

● The cooperation of county sports associations in finding assistant coaches.

● Many schools offered facilities free or at reduced rates.

● The heads of PE assisted with administration.

Weaknesses

● Lack of time limited the number of schools and sports included.

● In many cases, only those children able to arrange their own transport were able to attend the scheme.

Problems with other agencies

Heads of PE were put under considerable time pressure in dealing with administration.

New links

All the contacts with the school coaching centres were new, as were, more importantly, those with the PE staff, who have also come into contact with county sports associations.

Links are being made with many local clubs who will be looked upon to maintain coaching opportunities. These clubs are being linked to their local schools.

Contact has also been made with district sports development officers.

Scope for development

There needs to be detailed research into the needs of each sport, i.e. coaching courses, officials, equipment, etc., to help each sport structure a short-to-medium-term plan incorporating the aims of the project.

The number of sports and the number of centres, both at district and local level, need

to be increased to ensure improved accessibility.

There should be discussion with representatives of PE to work towards meeting the needs of the National Curriculum.

For long-term development, we are now looking closely at a programme of coach education, to ensure that schools and the community are prepared with a workforce of suitably qualified staff who are ready to continue the opportunity created by Champion Coaching.

The children

Sport	Sex	Age group	Ability level
Badminton	Mixed	11–14	Participation/performance
Basketball	Mixed	11–14	Participation/performance
Hockey	Mixed	11–14	Participation/performance
Netball	Girls	11–14	Participation/performance
Tennis	Mixed	11–14	Participation/performance

The coaches

Sport	No. children in squad	Head coaches	Assistant coaches	Ratio of coaches:children
Badminton*	6 + 13 + 9	1	-	1:6 / 1:3 / 1:9
	16	1	1	1:8
Basketball	9+24+7+20+12	1	-	1:9 / 1:24 / 1:7 / 1:20 / 1:12
Hockey	17 + 22 + 8	1	-	1:17 / 1:22 / 1:8
Netball	16 + 27 + 18	1	-	1:16 / 1:27 / 1:18
Tennis	15 + 7 + 6 + 9	1	-	1:15 / 1:7 / 1:6 / 1:9

*For example, a badminton School of Sport took place in four of the five districts involved in the scheme.

The facilities

Sport	Facility	Owned by	Hourly hire rate
Badminton	Sports halls (schools)	Northamptonshire County Council	Free / £10.00
Basketball	Sports halls (schools)	Northamptonshire County Council	Free / £10.00
Hockey	Pitches (schools)	Northamptonshire County Council	Free
	Pitch (club)	Kettering Hockey Club	Free
Netball	Sports hall (schools)	Northamptonshire County Council	Free
Tennis	Courts (schools)	Northamptonshire County Council	Free / £7.65 / £10.00
	Courts (club)	Old Grammarians	Free

Scheme

16

Peterborough Champion Coaching

Scheme Liaison Officer: Eric Robinson
Job title: [PE head of department, retired]
Scheme address:
c/o Education Department
Huntly Lodge
The Village
Orton Longueville
Peterborough
PE4 6UL
Telephone: 0733 371692

I feel that the most important factor by far in the success of Peterborough Champion Coaching has been the cooperation between the Cambridgeshire LEA and the Peterborough Council Leisure and Amenities Department. As the SLO I have had the considerable help of the Education (Inspectors) Department and its secretarial staff, spending many hours under their feet. The Leisure and Amenities Department's assistance has also been invaluable in finding facilities, negotiating days, times and costs, and providing contracts for assistant coaches ,as well as publicising the present scheme and starting negotiations for sponsorship for future schemes.

The Schools of Sport

The Schools of Sport ran once a week over a six-week period. All took place after school.

Children enrolled	149
Number of sessions	6
Potential attendances	894
Actual attendances	715
Percentage attendance	**80%**

Recruiting the children

A letter requesting nominations for the scheme was sent to the heads of PE at all the secondary schools in the Peterborough Local Education Authority. All schools were guaranteed one or two places per sport initially. The Scheme Liaison Officer selected children for any remaining places.

Choosing the children

Sport	Selection criteria
All	Those aged 12–14 years of school-team standard (but excluding those already involved in extra coaching for county squads, schools of excellence or similar), who are positive, enthusiastic and ready to commit themselves to the scheme.

How the scheme was managed

Major partners: Cambridgeshire Local Education Authority and Peterborough City Council Leisure and Amenities Department
Project managers: Graham Jones, Malcolm Groves (both General Inspectors, Cambridge Local Education Authority) and Gary Latham (Peterborough City Council Leisure and Amenities Department).

The Scheme Liaison Officer is employed by Cambridgeshire Local Education Authority.
Time spent on project: approximately 12 hours per week.

Management structure

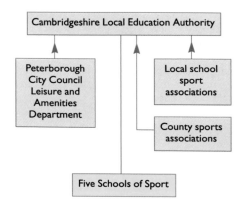

The children

Sport	Sex	Age group	Ability level
Badminton	Mixed	12–14	Performance
Cricket	Boys	12–14	Performance
Hockey	Mixed	12–14	Performance
Netball	Girls	12–14	Performance
Soccer	Mixed	12–14	Performance

The coaches

Sport	No. children in squad	Head coaches	Assistant coaches	Ratio of coaches:children
Badminton	25	1	2	1:8
Cricket	24	1	3	1:6
Hockey	36	1	4	1:7
Netball	25	1	3	1:6
Soccer	39	1	4	1:8

About the coaches

Two head and six assistant coaches were PE teachers.

Payment for assistant coaches: £22 per 90-minute session.

Minimum qualifications for assistant coaches: some involvement in playing and coaching the sport. Most coaches did have at least the preliminary coaching award of the national governing body.

Extra training provided: meetings were organised at which the head coaches discussed the coaching content of the course with the assistant coaches.

Transport

Parents provided the majority of the transport. A minibus, booked by the Scheme Liaison Officer, collected and returned pupils to those schools which required assistance.

Promoting the scheme

Leaflets and posters were circulated to all the secondary schools in Cambridgeshire Local Education Authority. The heads of PE were sent a letter outlining the scheme.

A launch was held, to which representatives of clubs, societies and cooperating agencies were invited.

All parents were notified by letter of their child's selection. They were encouraged to attend the coaching sessions and invited to the 'Young People in Sport' workshop.

The scheme was publicised in the local press and on local radio, and an attempt was made to have the scheme featured on regional television.

Additional funding

Contribution from children: none

How the money was spent

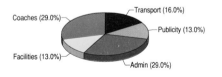

Coaches (29.0%)
Transport (16.0%)
Publicity (13.0%)
Facilities (13.0%)
Admin (29.0%)

Strengths of the scheme

● All schools in the authority were involved, giving a good social mix and establishing friendly and competitive relationships.

● We used first-class facilities and equipment.

● High-quality coaches.

● Cooperation of Peterborough Leisure and Amenities Department regarding the hire of facilities and contracts for assistant coaches.

● Use by the Scheme Liaison Officer of education office and secretarial staff.

● Cooperation of PE staff with Scheme Liaison Officer (ex-head of PE locally).

● Another major factor was the help given by the heads of PE departments of the local schools in providing youngsters of the correct standard of ability and attitude.

Weaknesses

● The amount of transport was limited because of cost, but mainly because of the difficulty of visiting every school within an hour either side of the School of Sport. Some youngsters were omitted through lack of transport.

● Some facilities were difficult to obtain, particularly leisure centres and public facilities during the early evening.

● Not all pupils who wanted a place could be accommodated.

Competition

No element of competition was included in the scheme.

New links

Working with the coaches has formed links with clubs. Local sports associations are all seeking recruits from the scheme for further coaching and teams.

Links with industry are proposed: for example, Pearl Assurance, via Peterborough City Council Leisure and Amenities Department Publicity and Promotions Officer.

Scope for development

It would be better for coaches to visit individual schools to cater for a smaller area before moving on to another area. This would mean less pupil transportation, more pupils could be accommodated, and some facilities could be guaranteed. We are seeking sponsorship for such a follow-up.

The Peterborough City Council Leisure and Amenities Department was coopted onto the scheme to help with expertise and contacts for future projects (mainly with regard to sponsorship).

All of the coaches are committed to the quality coaching ideals of Champion Coaching and many are already looking towards extending their coaching beyond this present scheme. I have already been asked to seek out possible venues and to enquire about costs to keep things 'on the boil'.

The facilities

Sport	Facility	Owned by	Hourly hire rate
Badminton	Sports hall (school)	Cambridgeshire County Council	£40 total
Cricket	Sports hall (leisure centre)	Peterborough City Council	£15.00
Hockey	Floodlit Astroturf (club)	Peterboro' Sports and Social Club	£15.00
Netball	Sports hall (leisure centre)	Peterborough City Council	£15.00
Soccer	Floodlit grass area	Peterborough City Council	£15.00

Scheme

17

RACE (Rydale Active Coaching Experience)

Scheme Liaison Officer: Mary Warden
Job title: RACE Coordinator
Scheme address:
Ryedale House
Malton
North Yorkshire
YO17 0HH
Telephone: 0603 600666

The Schools of Sport

The Schools of Sport ran once a week over an eight-week period. All took place after school.

Children enrolled	86
Number of sessions	8
Potential attendances	688
Actual attendances	647
Percentage attendance	**94%**

Recruiting the children

The PE staff of the four schools in the area selected the children for the scheme.

Choosing the children

Sport	Selection criteria
Basketball Hockey Soccer	Those with some ability, lots of enthusiasm and the will to take part, improve and achieve a high standard.

How the scheme was managed

Major partner: Rydale District Council
Project managers: RACE and Ryedale Sports Development.

The Scheme Liaison Officer is employed by Ryedale District Council. *Time spent on project:* 15 hours per week (designated).

Management structure

Ryedale District Council

Ryedale Sports Development Unit

Nine Schools of Sport

RACE is to run for three years with nine sports spread over the first year. We are a very rural area with only four secondary schools. It is very important that the children in this area can experience high-quality coaching on their doorstep, rather than having to travel the thirty miles or so to York, Teesside or Scarborough for it. We have brought coaches in from as far away as West Yorkshire to ensure that we give the best we can. The children have benefitted and have commented on how much they have enjoyed the courses. The scheme has helped us form partnerships with the schools, sports clubs and sports governing bodies which will be of great benefit for the future.

The children

	Sport	Sex	Age group	Ability level
Autumn term	Basketball	Mixed	12–16	Participation/performance
	Hockey	Mixed	12–16	Participation/performance
	Soccer	Mixed	12–16	Participation/performance
Spring term	Rugby league	Mixed	11–16	To be decided
	Rugby union	Mixed	11–16	
	Table tennis	Mixed	11–16	
Summer term	Badminton	Mixed	11–16	
	Cricket	Mixed	11–16	
	Tennis	Mixed	11–16	

The coaches

Sport	No. children in squad	Head coaches	Assistant coaches	Ratio of coaches:children
Basketball	29	1	1	1:15
Hockey	30	1	2	1:10
Soccer	27	1	1	1:14

Other agencies involved

North Yorkshire County Council Sports and Education Departments
North Yorkshire County Council Youth Service

About the coaches

So far, none of the head or assistant coaches have been PE teachers.

Payment per hour for assistant coaches: £7.50

Minimum qualifications for assistant coaches: to have, or to be working towards, the basic coaching qualification for the sport.

Coaches were recruited through governing bodies as we were unable to find them locally.

Extra training provided: none at present, but there are plans to provide coach education in the future.

Transport

Parents provided the majority of the transport. At one school, where parents could not provide it, the Scheme Liaison Officer and the Sports Development Officer helped out, and the Youth Service minibus was used.

Promoting the scheme

Promotion to schools and children was through headteachers, PE staff, posters in schools and articles in the press, where we stressed the value of the scheme.

After the children had been selected, letters were sent to their parents via the schools.

Additional funding

Ryedale District Council: £3650
North Yorkshire County Council: £2500

Contribution from children: £1 per two-hour session. This will give us an income of approximately £700 from the first three Schools of Sport.

How the money was spent

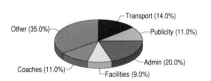

Other expenses: Scheme Liaison Officer salary, etc.

Strengths of the scheme

- Ryedale is a very rural area and the children have very few opportunities for sports coaching other than that offered by their school. The Champion Coaching Project gave them that opportunity.
- We knew that, being a rural area, we had many problems. The scheme has helped highlight these problems and so helped us to start solving them.
- Cooperation from PE staff.
- Willingness of parents to transport their children to and from the Schools of Sport.
- Full support from the Sports Development Officer.
- Help from governing bodies.

Weaknesses

- There was a lack of facilities; in this large rural area, we have no all-weather pitches and only one sports hall.
- Lack of public transport means we have to rely on parents. It would have been far too expensive to transport all the children otherwise.
- Because of a lack of local coaches, our coaches had to come from considerable distances — West Yorkshire in some cases.
- We lack large pools of equipment, and some courses had to go short because schools were not too keen to lend theirs and we did not have the funds to buy it.

Competition

The scheme contained no element of competition.

New links

The schools have never before been involved with the District Council or the governing bodies of sport, and Champion Coaching has created links between them.

Clubs are providing coaches and being used as exit routes, which has made them think more about provision for young people.

Problems with other agencies

We had some problems hiring the facilities at the times when we needed them.

Scope for development

We are running our scheme for three years and hope that over that time we will be able to establish top-quality coaching courses for young people by building on and improving the courses we have run. We hope to include some other sports and to open up the opportunities to more children. We also hope to offer holiday courses, as well as after-school courses. There are plans for coaching courses to encourage local people to become coaches.

Other comments

Ours has been a very good scheme. There have been lots of comments from the children about how much they have enjoyed the course. The first courses were too rushed and we needed more time for discussion with PE staff and to organise sports and venues better. It would have been better to have started in September since dark nights became a real problem.

Some coaches did not agree with the idea of picking out just one child for a fair play award.

The facilities

Sport	Facility	Owned by	Hourly hire rate
Basketball	Gymnasium (school)	North Yorkshire County Council	£10.00
Hockey	Pitch/gym/sports hall (school)	North Yorkshire County Council	£10.00
Soccer	Sports hall	Ryedale District Council	£17.50

Scheme

18

Sheffield Champion Coaching

Scheme Liaison Officer: Hugh Duff
Job title: Sports Development Manager
Scheme address:
Sheffield Recreation Department
North East Area Office
Tower Lodge
Firth Park Road
Sheffield
S5 6WS
Telephone: 0742 431253/431265

Sheffield City Council Recreation Department has been pioneering sports development work for over twelve years. The Sports Development Unit and Education Department secondary schools are already collaborating on the Sport and Young People Project, and the scheme has dovetailed perfectly into this by offering an opportunity to youngsters in schools to progress into the more structured coaching environment allowed for by Champion Coaching. Because of the size of Sheffield, its hills and valleys, and the consequent effect on travel, we set up two centres, the main one in the south of the city. Three facilities built for the World Student Games were used.

The Schools of Sport

The Schools of Sport ran once a week over a six-week period. They all took place after school.

Children enrolled	192
Number of sessions	6
Potential attendances	1152
Actual attendances	1002
Percentage attendance	**87%**

Recruiting the children

Each school in Sheffield was sent publicity material and was requested to nominate children for the scheme.

How the scheme was managed

Major partner and project manager: Sheffield Recreation Department

The Scheme Liaison Officer is employed by Sheffield City Council Recreation Department. *Time spent on project:* approximately 7 hours per week for ten weeks.

Choosing the children

Sport	Selection criteria
All	Those who have demonstrated to the teacher making the nomination a commitment to and reliability in school sport, and a willingness to practice their sport, who want to be involved in the scheme and are prepared to work hard at the Schools of Sport, who possess the basic skills of the sport, and who do not already represent their city or county or attend an advanced training centre or centre of excellence.

Management structure

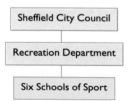

The children

Sport	Sex	Age group	Ability level
Badminton	Mixed	11–14	Performance
Basketball	Mixed	11–14	Performance
Hockey	Mixed	11–14	Performance
Netball	Girls	11–14	Performance
Rugby league	Mixed	11–14	Performance
Tennis	Mixed	11–14	Performance

The coaches

Sport	No. children in squad	Head coaches	Assistant coaches	Ratio of coaches:children
Badminton	34*	1	1	1:8
Basketball	35*	1	5	1:6
Hockey	51*	1	3	1:12
Netball	28	1	1	1:14
Rugby league	24	1	3	1:6
Tennis	20	1	1	1:10

*Two sites were used

About the coaches

One of the head coaches and three of the assistant coaches were PE teachers.

Payment per hour for assistant coaches: £5.00–£10.00

Minimum qualifications for assistant coaches: club coach award or similar.

Extra training provided: none

Transport

Transport was arranged informally by the children and the parents.

Promoting the scheme

All the schools in the area were sent publicity material and were requested to nominate children for the scheme. The scheme was also publicised in the local press. Clubs were contacted personally by the Scheme Liaison Officer and the coaches. Assistant coaches were found via contacts within the sport. Parents were invited to the 'Young People in Sport' Workshop.

Additional funding

Contribution from children: none

How the money was spent

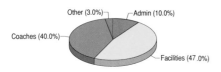

Other expenses: Additional T-shirts of the correct sizes.

Competition

Some internal competitions were included in the scheme.

Strengths of the scheme

● The high quality of the coaching ensured a high level of motivation on the part of the children.

● The fact that the Champion Coaching scheme was linked with the Sport and Young People project in Sheffield.

● It gave us the opportunity to offer youngsters a chance to use a number of the newly developed facilities in the city, such as the Don Valley Stadium.

● Some administrative support was already available.

Weaknesses

● We could not include some of the sports that we wanted as they were not selected for Champion Coaching Phase One.

New links

Although no new links have been formed, those already in existence have been strengthened.

Scope for development

Development of the scheme will require a continuation of resources. Structures need to be developed for participation, coaching and competition for young sportspeople.

Other comments

The scheme is worthwhile, but should be in addition to a well-organised and varied programme of school sport. The state of schools in Sheffield, and in particular their gymnasia, sports halls and playing fields, make it very difficult for such a basic programme to be successfully organised.

The facilities

Sport	Facility	Owned by	Hourly hire rate
Badminton	Sports hall (leisure centre)	Sheffield City Council	£12.00
	Sports hall (leisure centre)	Sheffield City Council	£11.00
Basketball	Sports hall (leisure centre)	Sheffield City Council	£12.00
	Sports hall (leisure centre)	Sheffield City Council	£11.00
Hockey	Sports hall (leisure centre)	Sheffield City Council	£11.00
	Pitch (club)	Abbeydale Sports Club	£30.00
Netball	Sports hall (leisure centre)	Sheffield City Council	£11.00
Rugby league	Don Valley Stadium	Sheffield for Health	£20.00
Tennis	Courts (leisure centre)	Sheffield City Council	£14.00

Scheme

19

Shropshire Champion Coaching

Scheme Liaison Officer: Martin Leath
Job title: Recreation Officer
Scheme address:
Winston Churchill Building
Radbrook Centre
Radbrook Road
Shrewsbury
Shropshire
SY3 9BJ
Telephone: 0743 254031

The Schools of Sport

The Schools of Sport ran once a week over a six-week period (eight weeks for swimming). Hockey and rugby union took place after school, the others in the evening. Rugby and table tennis have been extended.

Children enrolled	172
Number of sessions	6, 8
Potential attendances	1152
Actual attendances	922
Percentage attendance	**85%**

Recruiting the children

The PE staff in the schools selected the children from their school, although the head coaches may have recruited a small number of children that they had coached before.

Choosing the children

Sport	Selection criteria
All	Children of all abilities were allowed to apply, except for the table tennis at excellence level, where previous playing standards were taken into account.

How the scheme was managed

Major partner: Shropshire County Council
Project managers: Scheme Liaison Officer, head coaches.

The Scheme Liaison Officer is employed by Shropshire County Council Leisure Services. Time spent on project: 18 hours per week.

Other agencies involved

Local colleges

Among our successes has been the table-tennis School of Sport. This was held at the Grove School, Market Drayton, which boasts a host of championships, top players and coaches. The coaching ratio here was no higher than one to five, and the coaches were helped by Desmond Douglas. In addition, nearly twice as many boys applied for the rugby union School than expected, and Ian Taylor, the Great Britain goalkeeper, was the star guest at the last hockey session.

It is pleasing to report a clean bill of health for all the Schools of Sport, with no serious injury or accident, indicating skilful and and thoughtful coaching and management.

The children

Sport	Sex	Age group	Ability level
Hockey	Boys	13–14	Participation/performance
	Girls	13–14	Participation/performance
Rugby union	Boys	13–14	Performance
Swimming	Mixed	9–13	Participation/performance
Table tennis	Mixed	12–15	Excellence
	Mixed	13–14	Foundation

The facilities

Sport	Facility	Owned by	Hourly hire rate
Hockey	Artificial pitch (dual use)	Bridgnorth DC/Shropshire CC	£25.00
	Classroom (school)*	Shropshire County Council	£11.50
Rugby union	Pitch (school)	Shropshire County Council	£ 7.50
	Pitch (club)	Shrewsbury Rugby Club	£25.00
Swimming	Pool (dual use)	Nth Shropshire DC/Shropshire CC	£15.40
	Pool (dual use)	Wrekin DC/Shropshire CC	£20.00
	Pool (dual use)	Sth Shropshire CC/Shropshire CC	£18.00
Table tennis	Sports hall and gym (school)	Shropshire County Council	£20.00
	Sports hall (school)	Shropshire County Council	Free

*Hired for one hour-long session only.

Management structure

Shropshire County Council → Leisure Services → Six Schools of Sport

About the coaches

Five of the head coaches were ex-PE teachers or hold PE qualifications; four of the assistant coaches were PE teachers.

Payment per hour for assistant coaches: £7.50 (in addition, assistant coaches were paid 20p per mile for travel).

Minimum qualifications for assistant coaches: preliminary (level 1) awards, or ASA Advanced Teachers award for swimming.

Extra training provided: we provided no extra coaching during the actual scheme, but this has been identified as an urgent follow-up area.

Transport

Transport was normally informal. Additional transport was provided when the rugby course, for reasons of safety and for extra floodlighting, switched from Abraham Darby School to Shrewsbury Rugby Club. Shropshire Champion Coaching hired a private 52-seater minibus for the three sessions involved.

Promoting the scheme

The scheme was promoted in schools via PE and related teaching staff, with Champion Coaching posters and leaflets. Personal visits were also made to schools and clubs. We targeted private schools as well, and in fact recruited an assistant coach from a private school.

The children's parents were sent leaflets via the schools. The scheme was also featured in the local press.

A conference, Physical Education and Community Sport Partnership, to which all heads of PE and all Sports Development Officers were invited, was held in October 1991. The main speaker was Sue Campbell, Director of the National Coaching Foundation. Other speakers included Shropshire County Council's PE Adviser, David Penlington, and Chief Recreational Services Officer, Derek Haywood.

Additional funding

Contribution from children: either £10 or £15, but on all courses two free places were available for those children whose parents could not afford to pay.

How the money was spent

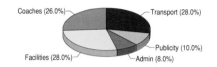

Coaches (26.0%) Transport (28.0%) Publicity (10.0%) Admin (8.0%) Facilities (28.0%)

Strengths of the scheme

- The availability and improvement of facilities. A new artificial pitch and floodlighting have helped the Shropshire scheme move forward.
- Established school links.
- Involvement of the Sports Development Officers, with sound local knowledge and administrative support.

Weaknesses

- The short timescale meant that some details were overlooked.
- The Schools of Sport may have been held too early in the evening, but this was dictated by the lack of public transport later at night in this very large rural county, and also the cost of facility hire at peak times.
- Other news in the local and national press and the fact that August is a 'lost month' in schools and local authorities, meant that there was a lack of major publicity.

Competition

Members of the boys' hockey course played a coached match against a county schools under-14 side.

New links

Although no new links were formed with schools, existing links have been improved. Support has been given to Grove Table Tennis Club and has possibly created a new table tennis club in Telford. We have also supported Bridgnorth Hockey Club, Shrewsbury Rugby Club and Ludlow Swimming Club.

We have also improved links with Sports Development Officers responsible for specific sports, the Sports Council and National Coaching Foundation Development Officers.

Problems with other agencies

There were no major problems, although many PE staff are already overloaded and were unable fully to promote the scheme.

Scope for development

The scheme could involve a wider range of sports, but development will require a longer planning and preparation period, greater contact with clubs as well as schools and colleges, more parental involvement, increased and continuous funding from central government, and improved education for assistant coaches.

A major sponsorship programme, run by Shropshire County Council and Wrekin District Council, may produce additional funding.

The coaches

Sport	No. children in squad	Head coaches	Assistant coaches	Ratio of coaches:children
Hockey	42	1	4	1:8
Rugby union	45	1	2	1:15
Swimming	60	1	5	1:10
Table tennis	25	1	4	1:5

Scheme

20

STEP (Sports Training towards Excellence and Performance)

Scheme Liaison Officer: Jane Knowles
Job title: STEP Project Officer
Scheme address:
East Dorset District Council
Furzehill
Wimborne
Dorset
BH21 4HN
Telephone: 0202 886201

STEP is an existing project into which Champion Coaching fitted well.

Sports science input by the Kerland Sports Services Team gave the scheme a unique feel. A multitude of physiological tests were carried out, each sport receiving a different test battery specific to it. Pre- and post-course testing was used. On the post-course test, the majority of the results significantly improved. I have put this down to greater motivation from the other squad members as the groups gelled — all were keen to improve their individual scores from the last time.

A video was made which is to be used as a teaching aid on the use of sports science in curriculum time.

The Schools of Sport

The Schools of Sport ran once a week for six to eight weeks. They all took place after school.

Children enrolled	94
Number of sessions	6, 7, 8
Potential attendances	694
Actual attendances	639
Percentage attendance	**92%**

Recruiting the children

A few schools were targeted around each venue or where the sport was strong. Letters were sent to headmasters and heads of PE giving information about the scheme. Children were mainly selected by their PE teachers, the criteria being deliberately loose so that the teachers could choose those children who would most benefit from and most enjoy the scheme. For the swimming school, clubs were asked to submit times for three boys and three girls in each age group.

Choosing the children

Sport	Selection criteria
Cricket	Those with enthusiasm to learn a new skill.
Hockey	Those playing for their school, but excluding county-level players.
Swimming	Rating on points system for each age-group, based on swimming times.
Table tennis	Those children who had played before and were enthusiastic.

How the scheme was managed

Major partner: East Dorset District Council
Project manager: Jane Knowles, STEP Project Officer

The Scheme Liaison Officer is funded by the Sports Council, British Petroleum and the local authorities. *Time spent on project:* 3–4 hours per week.

The children

Sport	Sex	Age group	Ability level
Cricket	Girls	11–14	Participation
Hockey	Mixed	12–14	Performance
Swimming	Mixed	11–14	Performance/excellence
Table tennis	Boys	12–14	Performance

The coaches

Sport	No. children in squad	Head coaches	Assistant coaches	Ratio of coaches:children
Cricket	14	1	1	1:7
Hockey	40	1	4	1:8
Swimming	24	1	1	1:12
Table tennis	14	1	2	1:5

The facilities

Sport	Facility	Owned by	Hourly hire rate
Cricket	Sports hall/nets (school)	Dorset County Council	£ 7.50
Hockey	Synth. pitch/spts hll (dual use)	Dorset CC/East Dorset DC	£10.00
Swimming	Pool/sports hall (school)	Dorset County Council	£18.22
Table tennis	Sports hall (school)	Dorset County Council	£ 8.33

Management structure

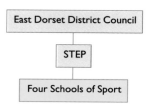

East Dorset District Council

STEP

Four Schools of Sport

Other agencies involved

County Youth Scheme

About the coaches

One head coach and four assistant coaches were PE teachers.

Payment per hour for assistant coaches: £7.50

Minimum qualifications for assistant coaches: all had governing body qualifications apart from two hockey coaches, who were PE teachers.

Extra training provided: none

Transport

Transport was mainly arranged informally by the children and their parents. Free transport was optional and all children were asked whether they required it. Only sixteen children took up the offer. In these cases transport was provided by taxi, paid for by Champion Coaching.

Promoting the scheme

The scheme was promoted to schools through letters, visits and talks at the area school sports associations, where the value of the scheme was stressed. Children were told about the scheme by their PE teachers. Clubs were sent letters and visited and coaches were contacted personally.

Other agencies were contacted through the local authorities' head of leisure. The schools which provided facilities were contacted through the headteacher.

Additional funding

Contribution from children: none

How the money was spent

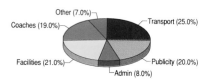

Other (7.0%)
Coaches (19.0%)
Transport (25.0%)
Facilities (21.0%)
Publicity (20.0%)
Admin (8.0%)

Other expenses: sports science support.

Strengths of the scheme

- All the participants were targeted individually. They therefore felt pride in gaining a place on the scheme.
- Good school links.
- The availability of good facilities and our ability to provide equipment.
- The ability to provide transport for participants when and where it was needed.
- At the swimming school of sport, parents supervised some of the land training, changing rooms, etc.

Weaknesses

- The fact that we did not charge the participating children a fee created a lack of respect for the course, and a lack of parental pressure to attend.

Competition

Some elements of competition were included within the Schools of Sport.

New links

The scheme has helped to cement the networks already established through the STEP Project.

Scope for development

In response to demand, another six-week swimming course has been set up to cater for three other clubs who declined to get involved the first time. In addition, an age-group squad has been formed which will meet on a regular basis.

The teachers who nominated the girls for the cricket course all attended the last Champion Coaching session. They have agreed to run internal competitions in their schools, with the STEP Project stepping in to run an external tournament in the summer term.

A junior table-tennis club and a regular weekly junior hockey session have been set up at the Champion Coaching venues, to commence in January. Coaches from the scheme are involved in both these projects.

Other comments

I did not feel that the PE teachers found the scheme to be a wonderful benefit. Though they were supportive, they felt it was yet another thing they had to get involved with. However, after the initial criteria-setting there was very little for them to do.

Scheme

21

St Edmundsbury Champion Choice

Scheme Liaison Officer: Justin Wallace
Job title: Leisure Development Officer
Scheme address:
St Edmundsbury Borough Council
Borough Offices
Angel Hill
Bury St Edmunds
Suffolk
IP3 1XB
Telephone: 0284 757085

The Schools of Sport

The Schools of Sport ran once a week over six-week period. All took place after school.

Children enrolled	180
Number of sessions	6
Potential attendances	1080
Actual attendances	1060
Percentage attendance	**98%**

How the scheme was managed

Major partner: St Edmundsbury Leisure Services Department
Project managers: Justin Wallace, Steve Harris and three Sports Development Officers.

The Scheme Liaison Officer is employed by St Edmundsbury Leisure Services Department. *Time spent on project:* 12 hours per week.

Management structure

St Edmundsbury Borough Council

Leisure Services

Assistant Chief Leisure Services Officer

Leisure Development Officer

Sports Development Officers

Five Schools of Sport

Have you ever watched a weightlifter start his lift? There is always a tremendous surge of power to overcome the weight's inertia. The bar seems to glide upwards with relative ease. For a local authority that had no sports development programme, the Champion Coaching Project was St Edmundsbury's power surge. Our scheme may have targeted only five sports for six weeks, but it was the catalyst that St Edmundsbury needed to set up a leisure development initiative. Our new ten-year programme will take sport to children from the age of one to the age of eighteen in four modules, with activities ranging from aerobics to abseiling.

Recruiting the children

The heads of PE at local feeder schools were given the selection criteria below and the recruitment was left to them. It was felt that they would be able to identify deserving children who had earned an opportunity to take part.

Choosing the children

Sport	Selection criteria
All	Those with a reasonable standard of coordination and interest in the sport, but excluding those already playing at high level (i.e. members of local clubs or local squads). We aimed at players in the second echelon who would benefit from expert coaching and would perhaps be interested in continuing in a club or class environment after the scheme.

About the coaches

Two head coaches and three assistant coaches were PE teachers.

Payment per hour for assistant coaches: £6.82

Minimum qualifications for assistant coaches: as laid down by the national governing bodies in the initial head coach selection documents.

Extra training provided: none

Transport

Transport was arranged informally by the children and their parents. St Edmundsbury Borough Council provided coaches to transport the children to the venues for the end-of-project competition.

Promoting the scheme

Posters were displayed in all the feeder schools and children were told about the scheme during assemblies.

Parents were informed about the scheme after their children had been selected. They were also invited to the 'Young People in Sport' workshop.

The value of the scheme was stressed throughout.

Additional funding

Contribution from children: none

How the money was spent

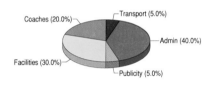

Coaches (20.0%)
Transport (5.0%)
Admin (40.0%)
Facilities (30.0%)
Publicity (5.0%)

Strengths of the scheme

- The prospect of clear exit routes at the end of the scheme. These are available because of the creation of the St Edmundsbury Leisure Development Initiative (SELDI).
- The high quality and ability of the head coaches.
- The cooperation between the PE teachers and the Sports Development Officers.
- The attention paid to detail by the Sports Development Officers.

Weaknesses

- The rural nature of the district made it difficult to reach all interested children, which meant that the numbers in each school were limited. However, this will be addressed in the Leisure Development Initiative.

Competition

In order to integrate the two schools (Bury St Edmunds and Haverhill), children were transported to the best venue for each sport to take part in an end-of-project competition. The standards of skill on show were more than adequate justification for the creation of the Champion Coaching Project.

New links

Champion Coaching has opened up tremendous opportunities for extra-curricular sports coaching in areas of weakness in schools.

Liaison with clubs through the Sports Council's Sportslink coordinator is becoming very positive.

New coaching contacts have resulted in a wider provision of course opportunities.

Scope for development

The creation of the St Edmundsbury Leisure Development Scheme Initiative (SELDI) means that there will be clear follow-up.

Other comments

Champion Coaching has been the catalyst that enabled St Edmundsbury to create SELDI. Without the grant from the National Coaching Foundation it would never have been approved. There is no doubt that without Champion Coaching the people of St Edmundsbury would not be looking forward to our exciting ten-year plan.

The children

Sport	Sex	Age group	Ability level
Badminton	Mixed	11–14	Foundation/participation
Basketball	Mixed	11–14	Foundation/participation
Hockey	Mixed	11–14	Foundation/participation
Soccer	Mixed	11–14	Foundation/participation
Table tennis	Mixed	11–14	Foundation/participation

The coaches

Sport	No. children in squad	Head coaches	Assistant coaches	Ratio of coaches:children
All	2 x 18	1	1	1:9

The facilities

Sport	Facility	Owned by	Hourly hire rate
Badminton	Sports hall (school)	Suffolk County Council	Free
	Sports hall (school)	Suffolk County Council	Free
Basketball	Sports hall (leisure centre)	St Edmundsbury Borough Council	£ 7.40
	Sports hall (school)	Suffolk County Council	Free
Hockey	Pitch	St Edmundsbury Borough Council	£10.00
	Sports hall (leisure centre)	St Edmundsbury Borough Council	£11.66
Soccer	Pitch	St Edmundsbury Borough Council	£10.00
	Sports centre	St Edmundsbury Borough Council	£11.66
Table tennis	Sports hall (school)	Suffolk County Council	£ 5.00
	Sports hall (school)	Suffolk County Council	Free

Scheme

22

Surrey Champion Coaching

Scheme Liaison Officer: Claire Holloway
Job title: Leisure Development Officer
Scheme address:
Surrey County Council
County Hall
Penrhyn Road
Kingston upon Thames
Surrey
KT1 2DN
Telephone: 081-541 9179

Photo: John Joannou

As a late entrant to the Champion Coaching Project, Surrey's task was to develop a high-quality scheme that was not only in line with national guidelines, but was also able to stand alone and be built onto in the future. Four sports were selected, each having already been identified as a priority for development. With the help of a dedicated steering group, the scheme was born. The scheme was based on two main distinctive principles: that after-school sport means exactly that — not evening or weekend sport; and that coaches are a valuable resource and should be paid. Hence all assistant coaches working on the scheme were paid in line with governing-body guidelines.

The Schools of Sport

The Schools of Sport ran once a week over a six-week period. They all took place after school.

Children enrolled	128
Number of sessions	6
Potential attendances	768
Actual attendances	645
Percentage attendance	**84%**

Recruiting the children

In September, nomination forms and criteria for selection were sent to heads of PE, asking for a response by early October. This was followed up by a chasing letter in early October. In mid-October, owing to a poor response from middle schools, additional secondary schools were approached. The coaches and PE Inspectors vetted the application forms.

Choosing the children

Sport	Selection criteria
Cricket Netball Tennis	Those who show interest in and promise at the chosen sport, who would respond to and benefit from more specialised coaching, who possess the motivation and self-discipline to develop their ability, and who can confirm their commitment to continue beyond the scheme by joining a club.
Rugby union	As above, but, because of initial poor response, widened to include players at participation level.

How the scheme was managed

Major partner: Surrey County Council
Project managers (Steering Group):
Claire Holloway (Leisure Development Manager (SCC))
Tony Pannell (PE Adviser (SCC))
Pauline Fancourt (South East Regional Sports Council)
Peter Brett (Administrator, Surrey County Youth Cricket Trust)
Andy Challis (Rugby Football Union Youth Development Officer)
Jean Thirwall (Lawn Tennis Association County Development Officer)
Rachel Foley (Surrey County Netball Association)

The Scheme Liaison Officer is employed by Surrey County Council. *Time spent on project:* 10 hours per week (averaged over June to November, but probably 36 hours per week in October!)

Management structure

Other agencies involved

Surrey County Cricket Club

The children

Sport	Sex	Age group	Ability level
Cricket	Mixed*	11–14	Performance
Netball	Girls	11–14	Performance
Rugby union	Mixed	11–14	Participation/performance
Tennis	Mixed	11–14	Performance

*Only boys applied

About the coaches

One head coach and two assistant coaches were PE teachers. In addition, one head coach was an ex-PE teacher.

Payment per hour for assistant coaches: £14 (including expenses).

Minimum qualifications for assistant coaches: national governing body preliminary award together with experience of working with children. Where possible, assistant coaches were drawn from local clubs so that they could help with the exit routes.

Extra training provided: the National Coaching Foundation course Coaching Children was offered to all assistant coaches, but none took it.

Transport

Transport problems were avoided by drawing pupils only from local schools. Schools were responsible for transporting children to the venue and parents were asked to collect them.

Promoting the scheme

Letters were sent by the PE Inspector to all headteachers and heads of PE. Children were informed via their PE teachers and posters.

Press releases appeared in the local papers.

A 'debriefing' session was held for parents and participants after each individual school of sport. This involved a short talk by the PE Inspector and chief coach, a question and answer session, and distribution of Champion Coaching Parent Packs. These sessions worked well, were well attended and parents showed a keen interest in the scheme.

Additional funding

Surrey County Council: £2500

Contribution from children: none

How the money was spent

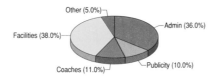

Other (5.0%) — Admin (36.0%)
Facilities (38.0%)
Coaches (11.0%) — Publicity (10.0%)

Other expenses: contribution to seminar on club-school liaison.

Strengths of the scheme

- Strong support of the Education Department and representatives of the sports. Presence of the PE Inspector, development officers from cricket, hockey and rugby, and the netball chief coach on steering group.

- Strong support from the two sports centres used. These are dual-use centres with close relations between school PE staff and sports-centre staff.

Weaknesses

- The PE staff were not given adequate time to advertise the scheme and select the children. As a result, we had to do a 'hard sell' at the last minute to get numbers up — and ended unable to ensure a balanced spread of age, sex, etc. The timescale for the introduction of Champion Coaching was far too short. Autumn term is not a good time to run coaching courses through schools, as staff are already bogged down with start-of-year paperwork.

Competition

Children from the netball School of Sport took part in a competition at the London Playing Fields Association ground. We are hoping to arrange a similar competition for the cricketers in the spring.

New links

Links already existed with schools, but links between the schools themselves and between them and the four sports have begun to form.

Links have been formed with Camberley Rugby Club and Frimley Star Tennis Club, and we will also link into several cricket clubs.

Photo: John Joannou

Scope for development

The scheme could be developed by increasing the number of schools of sport and by using additional centres to expand the scheme into other parts of the county.

The Abbeylands centre is already planning a sports workshop, to take place in March, for clubs, headteachers and heads of PE, and we hope to do something similar in the Tomlinscote area.

Other comments

The enthusiastic response suggested that the majority of course participants will continue their interest in their chosen sport through the local club network and that parents welcome the Champion Coaching initiative. We look forward to being part of it in the future.

The coaches

Sport	No. children in squad(s)	Head coaches	Assistant coaches	Ratio of coaches:children
Cricket	32	1	1*	1:16
Netball	38	1	2*	1:13
Rugby union	40	1	2	1:13
Tennis	18	1	1	1:9

*Visiting specialists also acted as assistant coaches on some occasions.

The facilities

Sport	Facility		Owned by	Hourly hire rate
Cricket	Sports hall	(dual use)	Surrey CC/Runnymede BC	£15.00*
Netball	Sports hall			£15.00*
	Floodlit hard court			£12.50
Rugby union	Sports hall	(dual use)	Surrey CC/Runnymede BC	£16.40
Tennis	Hard court			£11.60

*£17.50 after 6pm.

Scheme

23

The Three Cs (Carlisle Champion Coaching)

Scheme Liaison Officer: Andy Bradbury
Job title: Assistant Client Officer
Scheme address:
Leisure Services Department
Civic Centre
Carlisle
Cumbria
CA3 8QG
Telephone: 0228 23411 ext. 2510

The Schools of Sport

The Schools of Sport ran once a week over a six-week period. They all took place after school.

Children enrolled	144
Number of sessions	6
Potential attendances	864
Actual attendances	842
Percentage attendance	**97%**

Recruiting the children

Each secondary school was allocated a certain number of places for each sport, dependent on the sports played at the school and the roll number. Children were selected by the PE staff. Following selection, children were sent a letter giving details of the course and transport.

Choosing the children

Sport	Selection criteria
Swimming	Those currently swimming for a school or club team.
Table tennis	13–14-year-olds who have some experience of playing table tennis at school or with a club.
Others	13–14-year-olds who are currently playing for the school team and who show a talent that could be improved with coaching.

How the scheme was managed

Major partner: Carlisle City Council
Project managers: Carlisle City Council, Andy Bradbury, Jim Crowe, Gary Schubert.

The Scheme Liaison Officer is employed by Carlisle City Council Leisure Services. *Time spent on project:* 10 hours per week.

The major consideration in planning our scheme was its continuation after the six weeks. Perhaps the most important factor in having a good-quality scheme was the coaches and their assistants. Once they have built up a rapport with the children, it would be a great shame to break it up. In order to obtain this continuity it was decided that both the head coaches and their assistants should come from the pool of coaches locally available. This also has the benefit of building further links between clubs and schools, already initiated through our Sportslink 90 scheme; this will provide great long-term benefits, and should result in clubs running sessions at the schools.

The children

Sport	Sex	Age group	Ability level
Hockey	Mixed	13–14	Performance/excellence
Netball	Girls	13–14	Performance/excellence
Rugby league	Boys	13–14	Performance/excellence
Soccer	Boys	13–14	Performance/excellence
Swimming	Mixed	11–14	Performance/excellence
Table tennis	Mixed	13–14	Performance

The coaches

Sport	No. children in squad	Head coaches	Assistant coaches	Ratio of coaches:children
Hockey	25	1	1	1:12
Netball	27	1	2	1:13
Rugby league	17	1	1	1:8
Soccer	25	1	1	1:12
Swimming	30	1	1	1:15
Table tennis	20	1	4	1:4

Management structure

Carlisle City Council → Leisure Services → Six Schools of Sport

Other agencies involved

Cumbria County Council

The coaches

None of the head coaches were PE teachers; two of the assistant coaches were.

Payment per hour for assistant coaches: £6.25

Minimum qualifications for assistant coaches: to have completed the National Coaching Foundation *Coaching Children* course and to be actively involved with coaching in clubs or schools.

Extra training provided: National Coaching Foundation *Coaching Children* course.

Transport

All children were transported to the coaching schemes if required and returned to their schools. Transport was paid for out of the budget and was provided by coaches and taxis hired for the job.

Promoting the scheme

A letter to the schools was followed by a visit to the heads of PE, when the value of the scheme was emphasised. PE teachers informed the children. Parents of the selected children were informed by letter.

Clubs were approached through the coordinator of the existing Sportslink 90 scheme.

Funding

Carlisle City Council: £2300

Contribution from children: none

How the money was spent

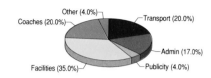

Other (4.0%), Coaches (20.0%), Transport (20.0%), Admin (17.0%), Publicity (4.0%), Facilities (35.0%)

Other expenses: launch and coaches' meetings.

Strengths of the scheme

- All the coaches are attached to local clubs, which means they will all be available for follow-up sessions, and will provide a school-club link.

- The existence of the Sportslink 90 scheme, which is currently running, and is aimed at providing a link between local sports clubs and schools, to encourage the continuation of sports participation.

- The existence of a Development Officer for rugby league and hockey.

- The availability of school facilities for use by the scheme.

- The help received from the PE staff in the schools.

Weaknesses

- The nine secondary schools in Carlisle are spread over a large area. This caused problems in transport and timing of sessions. It would probably have been better to have involved fewer schools in the initial project.

- The low level of County Council involvement. In the long run, it would probably have been advantageous to have obtained more help from within the County Council system.

Competition

No element of competition was included within the Schools of Sport.

New links

The scheme has provided contacts with the heads of PE and PE teachers; that contact had not really been happening before. This also stimulated an interest in after-school sport on the part of the heads of PE.

The scheme has used coaches from all the local clubs, and has worked in conjunction with the Sportslink 90 scheme to strengthen the links between club and school.

Scope for development

The Schools of Sport are to be repeated in Phase Two, but at the foundation, participation and performance levels. The scheme could be extended to provide after-school coaching sessions at individual schools, rather than trying to bring everybody into a central session. This would considerably reduce the problems of

transport. Ideally, we would have provided the sessions that each school required at that school.

The facilities

Sport	Facility	Owned by	Hourly hire rate
Hockey	Sports hall (school)	Cumbria County Council	£10.00
Netball	Sports hall (school)	Cumbria County Council	£15.00
Rugby league	Pitch	Carlisle City Council	£30.00
Soccer	Pitch	Carlisle City Council	£30.00
Swimming	Pool (school)	Cumbria County Council	£35.00
Table tennis	Sports hall (school)	Cumbria County Council	£15.00

Scheme

24

Windsor and Maidenhead Champion Coaching

Scheme Liaison Officer: Sean Kearns
Job title: Recreation Development Officer
Scheme address:
Aston House
York Road
Maidenhead
SL6 1PS
Telephone: 0628 796289

The Schools of Sport

The Schools of Sport ran once a week over seven-week period. They all took place after school, except one soccer school, which was at the weekend.

Children enrolled	157
Number of sessions	7
Potential attendances	1099
Actual attendances	934
Percentage attendance	**85%**

Choosing the children

Sport	Selection criteria
Soccer	Those having reached level 4* Coca Cola Award.
Others	None — self-selection.

How the scheme was managed

Major partner: Royal Borough Council of Windsor and Maidenhead Recreation Unit
Project managers: Recreation Development Team

The Scheme Liaison Officer is employed by the Royal Borough of Windsor and Maidenhead Borough Council. *Time spent on project:* 6 hours per week.

Management structure

Royal Borough of Windsor and Maidenhead Borough Council

Berkshire County Council

Recreation Development Team

Eight Schools of Sport

We are especially pleased to have made our contribution to this national initiative. Our success has been the development of a permanent network, consisting of local coaches, schools, clubs and the local authority, which will continue to provide high-quality sessions beyond Champion Coaching Phase One. We are establishing a training network, to be coordinated by the local sports council, to overcome the shortage of experienced and qualified coaches available for after-school coaching.

Phase Two will see the Champion Coaching initiative developed to provide an extended after-school coaching programme for junior residents of the Borough.

Recruiting the children

An advertisement appeared for three weeks in the local press. Children interested in the scheme were asked to approach either their head of PE or the Leisure Services Department directly (which the majority did).

About the coaches

Two of the head coaches were ex-PE teachers; none of the assistant coaches were PE teachers.

Payment per hour for assistant coaches: £7.50

Minimum qualifications for assistant coaches: national governing body minimum preliminary award.

Extra training provided: none

The children

Sport	Sex	Age group	Ability level
Badminton	Mixed	11–14	Participation
	Mixed	11–14	Participation
Netball	Girls	11–14	Performance
Rugby union	Mixed	11–15	Participation
Soccer	Boys	11–14	Participation
	Boys	11–14	Participation/performance
Tennis	Mixed	11–14	Participation
	Mixed	11–14	Participation/performance

Transport

Transport was arranged informally by the children and their parents. No additional transport was required.

Promoting the scheme

An advert was run in the press, PE teachers were written to, the PE roadshow visited the schools, and posters were displayed in schools and clubs.

After the selection of their child, parents were informed by phone or letter and were also sent questionnaires.

The importance of after-school sport was stressed in a full-page article which appeared in both local papers following interviews with the sports editors. A video was made in conjunction with Windsor Cable TV, featuring the Schools of Sport and interviews, including one with the Minister for Sport.

Additional funding

Contribution from children: children, except those in the rugby union School of Sport, were asked to pay a fee for each session. The fees were: soccer (Windsor) and netball: £1.00; badminton, soccer (Maidenhead) and tennis: £1.50. The total collected was £800.

How the money was spent

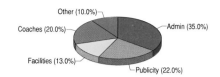

Other expenses: future training in Jan–Mar 1992.

Strengths of the scheme

- The administration and organisation was made easier by the existence of an established development scheme.

- Both head and assistant coaches have taken the initiative to their hearts and want to succeed. Important too has been their ability to adapt and improvise.

- The willingness of schools to participate in the scheme.

Weaknesses

- The current programme was restricted because of the lack of floodlit facilities.

- Child selection was difficult. We had a large response from the advertising and initial criteria were not always met. We ended up with mixed-ability groups.

Competition

Some elements of competition were included within the Schools of Sport.

New links

Lynne Ellis, in her role as Partnership Officer in the Recreation Development team, has benefitted from the scheme in that she has forged new links, especially with schools. There have been limited new links with clubs.

A employment network of coaches has been formed, based on quality delivery. The coaches discussed their problems, and helped each other across the sports.

Problems with other agencies

There were some minor difficulties with one or two schools.

Scope for development

The current programme could be extended to provide for the demand at the foundation, participation and performance levels.

The coaches

Sport	No. children in squad(s)	Head coaches	Assistant coaches	Ratio of coaches:children
Badminton	11 + 18	1 + 1	2 + 3	1:4 / 1:5
Netball	35	1	5	1:6
Rugby union	18	1	1	1:9
Soccer	22 + 13	1 + 1	1 + 2	1:11 / 1:4
Tennis	22 + 18	1 + 1	3 + 2	1:5 / 1:6

The facilities

Sport	Facility	Owned by	Hourly hire rate
Badminton	Sports hall (school)	Berkshire County Council	Free
	Sports hall (school)	Berkshire County Council	£10.00
Netball	Sports hall (leisure centre)	Borough Council	Free (7 weeks)
Rugby union	Pitch (club)	Home Park WRFC/Borough Council	£ 7.00 / free
Soccer	Pitch (school)	Berkshire County Council	£ 5.00
	Pitch (club)	Maidenhead RFC/Borough Council	£12.50
	Pitch (school)	Berkshire County Council	£ 5.00
Tennis	Courts (school)	Berkshire County Council	£ 5.00
	Courts (leisure centre)	Borough Council	Free
	Courts (club)	Windsor Lawn Tennis Club	£ 5.00

Close-up on Bradford

Background

Bradford is a Yorkshire industrial town with a tradition of producing keen cricketers and ferocious rugby players. And although its Recreation Department doesn't spend much of its budget on shouting about it, there is also a well-established and effective Council programme for encouraging many types of sport at many levels. There is a considerable social and ethnic mix in and around the town, with a particular concentration of families with origins in the Indian sub-continent.

Deiniol Williams is Bradford Metropolitan Council's Project Coordinator for Sport and Young People, and he was clearly the best person to set up their Champion Coaching scheme.

Deiniol obviously loves his job, which keeps him in close contact with everybody involved with youth and sport in Bradford and the nearby towns which make up the Metropolitan District. It only takes a few minutes with him to start to catch his enthusiasm. He's committed to encouraging participation: 'A generation or so ago, it was sport or nothing, but young people these days have so many ways to occupy themselves — particularly TV — that in a way there is a need to redress the balance.'

The project he runs was set up in 1990. It has developed good information systems to co-ordinate the sport interests of schools, youth clubs, police and the probation service. Deiniol has a reasonable amount of freedom to operate, and is able to make rapid decisions — a tremendous advantage when the prospect of Champion Coaching, with its very tight schedules, was first mentioned to him by the Sports Council's Phil Wagner. 'We had to go through all the hurdles of applying for it' said Deiniol 'but most of the systems we needed were already there. My concern was not just that we should get the scheme, but that we would be able to follow it up in the future — I don't want this to be a one-shot effort.'

Practical considerations

Realism marked Bradford's approach to Champion Coaching at all stages. Six sports were chosen (cricket, hockey, rugby union, soccer, swimming and tennis), partly because of local popularity and partly because they were suited to existing facilities and had Development Officers active within the area. Of these, hockey, swimming and tennis are mixed, the others being for boys only. Because of ethnic customs, mixed sport needs sensitive handling in some parts of Bradford.

The Council's own sports centres were used, and children were drawn from schools local to the appropriate centre — this disposed of the transport difficulties that a wider approach would have involved. It was also calculated to lessen the drop-out rate as the evenings became dark towards the end of the scheme. It was necessary to provide a small amount of assistance with transport. Goodwill, ingenuity and the sharing of taxis on tight contracts kept the cost of this down to only about £200 overall. As Deiniol said, this was a last resort: first you have to prove that walking, public transport or helpful parents are not practical alternatives.

Selecting the children

More than 40 schools were visited during the selection process. Bradford's children go to lower, middle and upper schools, the age ranges being 5–9 years, 9–13 and 13–18. As the ChampionCoaching range is 11–14, children were drawn from both middle and upper schools. This would have presented problems in the case of cricket, which was therefore confined to 13–14-year-old children, from upper schools only.

For swimming, most of the children were chosen from those who had performed fairly well at the 1991 Bradford Schools' Championships, but were not good enough to enter the established coaching schemes. For the other sports, the recruits were all participants already, but not top performers.

Bradford's strengths

Deiniol gives full credit to Bradford Council's attitude to encouraging sport and to the existing infrastructure when talking about how Bradford Champion Coaching had got going without any serious snags. For most of the sports there were already Development Officers, and they played a major part in the organisation. He had a lot of freedom to make decisions without having to go through time-consuming committees. He had also already established good relationships with schools in the area, so there was less suspicion from teachers than might otherwise have been the case.

Summing up

Apart from the obvious effects of extra good-quality coaching in the City, Deiniol Williams welcomed Champion Coaching for three main reasons:

- It would bring in some new equipment
- It would bring in some new coaches
- It would provide an opportunity to emphasise what good facilities and coaching schemes already existed in the area.

So far, he is happy that all these benefits have been realised. His only question now is: What next for Champion Coaching in Bradford?

Launching the Bromley scheme

Background

Bromley is the largest of the London Boroughs. It fills a great stretch of South-east London and spills over the Kentish border. Much of it is prosperous commuter-land, with many sports clubs and open spaces, but there are also some relatively depressed areas. There is a higher proportion of independent schools than in many other areas, and many of these are still single-sex.

Bromley's Leisure Services operate a vigorous Sports Development Unit, masterminded by Bernie Hamill, the Manager, from the Council Offices in the centre of town. Bernie first heard about the Champion Coaching scheme early in May, via her local Sports Council contact.

Practical considerations

Like Deiniol in Bradford, Bernie had no difficulty in persuading her department that Champion Coaching was a good idea. The infrastructure was there, and the Council was committed to promoting active lifestyles. Some sports already had a good history of partnership with the community, and were natural choices for Champion Coaching. Soccer, based on Crystal Palace, was typical of these. Six sports were chosen in all: basketball, cricket, hockey, netball, soccer and tennis, each based on a single venue.

Because of the high anticipated demand, two or three Schools of Sport were established for each sport, some after school, some on Saturday mornings. This meant that the Champion Coaching resources were thinned out a bit, but more children were able to take part. They all received either a *SportLog* or a T-shirt, but not both.

Basketball and netball were for boys and girls respectively, with all the other sports being mixed.

Selecting the children

Bromley's schools are divided into primary (up to 11) and secondary. Children in the scheme were all drawn from the secondary schools. All the schools in the Borough were invited to participate.

All the recruits were already participants in the sports who had shown some ability but were not of school first-team or county-team standard. Announcements were made in all the schools, and recruitment was on a first-come, first-served basis.

Generally, no special transport was provided, and schools and parents were encouraged to co-operate as much as possible to ensure that the children could get to the sessions. In one or two cases, a team minibus was able to be pressed into service.

More children wanted to take part than could be accommodated. In netball, the pressure from parents was so great that an extra scheme is to run on after Champion Coaching 1991 has officially finished.

Snags and criticisms

Time! Bernie found the tight time-scale of this first Champion Coaching scheme was a big problem, particularly as school holidays came right in the middle of the preparation period. A further slight snag was that half-term holidays fell during the Schools of Sport, but after due consideration it was decided to ignore these and continue straight through once the Schools of Sport had got under way.

Finding a sufficient number of coaches was a problem in some sports — this was particularly the case with netball.

Although reasonable pay was given to the assistant coaches (in Bromley they received £10.70/hr), Bernie felt that they needed something else, such as kit, to identify them more with the scheme.

The sessions at the Schools of Sport were scheduled to take 1½ hours each; with the benefit of hindsight, Bernie says that she would have tried to extend this, perhaps to 2 hours, to allow longer for session review and entering data in the *SportLogs*.

Bromley's strengths

Bromley had a strong team of sports development personnel already in place at the start of the scheme, and Bernie freely

acknowledges that this was largely responsible for its success. 'Teamwork is the key', she says. She felt that her own experience in teaching had also helped her in liaising with the schools.

Summing up

Bernie knows that Champion Coaching has been very well received in the Borough, and would like to keep the scheme and the name alive. She is not sure about the wisdom of running it for many sports simultaneously again — she suggests a rolling programme of the sports in season.

Can Bromley organise it again? Of course! 'If you've done it once, you can do it again' is Bernie's positive comment.

The Main Ingredients

*Comparison and analysis
of the schemes*

This chapter outlines the chief ingredients of Champion Coaching, and synthesises the lessons learned for future endeavours.

One benefit of a nationally coordinated after-school sport initiative is that comparisons can be made across the board. We have been able to interpret and evaluate the schemes centrally, and to act as a clearing house for policy and practical guidance. Champion Coaching has not only allowed us to sing the praises of quality after-school sport, it has enabled us all to sing from the same hymn book.

Parents, coaches, organisers and children get together in Blackburn

Major partners: the delivering agencies

When we considered potential schemes for inclusion in the project, there were no specific profiles for the agencies that would deliver the Schools of Sport. Instead, the 24 selected partners were chosen on their perceived overall ability to meet the national criteria listed on page 8.

Each scheme also had to be endorsed by the Champion Coaching Project Coordinator and the Regional Sports Council Director.

When the final selection was made, the breakdown of agencies across the country was:

Borough councils	7
County councils	6
City councils	5
Local education authorities	2
District councils	1
Joint partners	3*

*2 borough councils, a local education authority with a city council, and a district council with a regional Sports Council

No one partner model outshines the rest, because the Champion Coaching schemes were designed, developed and delivered to match the existing structures.

Although the national policy package was moulded to complement and supplement local needs and abilities, it was not rewritten. The 24 schemes were created to carry out a consistent approach to after-school sport. The abilities of all the agencies to deliver the national game plan are now being evaluated.

One advantage of working to a tight timescale was the necessity to identify agencies which had the flexibility to inject new and exciting priorities into their current work programmes. Champion Coaching worked with enterprising people who were willing to take risks to improve their communities' provision for after-school sport.

Within the six types of agency there were three main factors that contributed to the overall effectiveness of the delivery package. They were:

● *Support staff:* administrative help was critical in the organisation and timely implementation of each scheme

● *The Scheme Liaison Officer's expertise:* the look and tone of a scheme invariably mirrored the capabilities of the SLO. Their strengths became the project's strengths.

● *The sport development unit's vision:* eleven schemes were in areas with established sport development units that could be pressed into action for Champion Coaching. The existence of these sport development units did not necessarily guarantee the quality of the delivering agency. However, when the unit contained experienced, committed officers with a shared vision, we did find that the children were treated to very special Schools of Sport.

Management structures: local accountability

Some schemes already had a management structure in place, or developed one specifically for Champion Coaching. There were three basic types:

● *Internal,* where there existed an internal advisory group that at the least was kept informed about progress and at most was the decision-making board to which the SLO answered locally.

● *External,* where an advisory group was created with representatives outside the delivering agency who came from the various networks required to host an effective programme.

● *Lone Wolf,* where the SLO had a line manager within his/her agency but did not answer to any advisory committee for Champion Coaching.

Here are two excellent Lone Wolf examples:

Coventry — Andy Wright

Despite becoming a SLO later than most, and lacking extensive agency or secretarial support, Andy:

• established his own local news-letter to improve communication with schools and teachers

• organised several orientation meetings for coaches

• worked tirelessly to attend and oversee the coaching sessions

Although Andy worked single-handedly from his school office, he was able to draw on the patterns established by the long-term Coventry Active Lifestyles Project.

London Playing Fields Society — Alex Walsh

Alex is in charge of facility use and sport development at a large complex. He has made a huge impact on local sport, giving a lead to the community in starting to coordinate the various competitive structures for children. He was one of two SLOs who were also head coaches; despite the disadvantages of combining two roles, this helped establish an excellent rapport with the other coaches, for he knew their problems from the inside.

In the 1991 Champion Coaching project there were outstanding schemes from each of the above groups. It would have been an added and unnecessary burden to require the very capable Lone Wolves to create a committee structure. Likewise, where either an external or internal management structure existed it was used to good advantage.

However, for the long-term role of Champion Coaching as a valued member of the sporting community it must have direct links with its contributing networks. A small, well-informed and dedicated advisory committee for each scheme could be the forum needed to debate such issues as which sports to choose, where to schedule sessions, how to select children in the performance band, and how to ensure that there are stable exit routes. This first phase of Champion Coaching attempted to mesh with children's needs in the local community. If the project is to reach its full potential in leading after-school sport, it must draw together a coalition of networks which are willing to use Champion Coaching as a platform upon which to work together.

One management variable that enhanced the design and delivery of seven of the Champion Coaching schemes was the outstanding support given by three regional Sports Council offices. Although all ten regions ably assisted in the selection process, it was not always possible or practical for regional offices to monitor the progress of local schemes. However, the Northern Region (Carlisle and Middlesbrough), the Eastern Region (Chelmsford, Peterborough and St Edmundsbury), and the Southern Region (Hampshire and Windsor and Maidenhead) worked beyond the call of duty to provide patient and tactful guidance from their senior regional officers. With their help the Champion Coaching schemes were enhanced most significantly by fitting into a total area outlook from start to finish.

Some local authorities had already established a responsible management post within their leisure departments which was equivalent to Youth Sport Coordinator (see end of third column on this page). Where this was the case, once the postholder had become convinced of the value of the programme, it made the introduction of Champion Coaching particularly smooth. The Bromley scheme was a good example of this.

> *After-school sport plays an important part in the healthy growth and development of children, yet it is undergoing enormous changes. In this atmosphere of change it is often difficult to say who funds, who organises, who directs and who monitors after-school sports activities.*
>
> [Champion Coaching information leaflet, June 1991]

The Scheme Liaison Officer — tomorrow's Youth Sport Coordinator

Knowing the sea of possibilities and complex routes that one could encounter, it was critical for the national Project Coordinator, Katie Donovan, to have a direct line of communication with one voice in each scheme. Accordingly, Champion Coaching listed as one of its main entry qualifications that a competent and caring professional must be appointed to direct each local scheme. The Scheme Liaison Officers became the right arm of the central office in Leeds.

Without question, the ultimate quality of each of Champion Coaching's 24 schemes rested squarely on the shoulders of the Scheme Liaison Officers. Who are they?

● They range from 23 years old to 63 years old.

● Some were in full-time employment, some were self-employed, and some had already retired.

● They are generally from physical education and leisure services backgrounds.

● At one extreme they are ex-international athletes, at the other they are almost non-movers.

● They are current coaches, ex-coaches and non-coaches.

● They are sports scientists, teachers, principal officers, leisure centre managers, sport development officers and physical education advisors.

Endless comparisons could be made about the strengths and weaknesses of the above categories, but without any hope of drawing consistent conclusions. It's all down to people, so let's look at a profile of the skills that the SLOs, the cooperating networks, the monitoring and evaluation team and the Project Coordinator found are needed to get the after-school sport job accomplished, regardless of academic qualifications or parent agency:

1 Professional and personal commitment to the improvement of young people's sport

2 Thorough knowledge of the local community, including schools and teachers, volunteer agencies, clubs, local authorities, governing bodies, and sport-specific development officers

3 Credibility within the community and a majority of its networks

4 Strong presentation and negotiating skills

5 Capable in the management of people, finances and facilities

6 An enthusiastic acceptance of their 'agent of change' role and the inevitable conflict that goes with the job

Youth Sport Coordinators

One of the clearest lessons of Champion Coaching is that to have consistent, quality-controlled after-school sport for young people, there must be a national policy and vision that is acted out by strong and competent Youth Sport Coordinators operating in the best interests of children.

Three major points when discussing the future of Youth Sport Coordinators are:

- Potential YSCs already exist, but they need a clear focus and direct accountability to a national programme if they are to be effective.

- YSCs are not to be confused with less experienced Sport Development Officers. The YSC represents experience and expertise within a system. They should be capable of coordinating and leading communities for the overall benefit of many sports and all the children, not merely creating opportunities in a single sport.

- Now is the time to work with higher education to begin to train future YSCs, with curriculum modules for PE and community management courses.

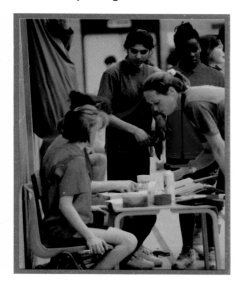

The right person, given adequate time, funding and authority, can move mountains in the complicated and often uncoordinated arena of school-age sport. At present the recruitment, training and employment of outstanding Youth Sport Coordinators is the largest single factor for improving quality opportunities for children.

The coaches

The 136 Champion Coaching head coaches were effective quality control agents.

The task of putting Champion Coaching's policy into practice was the responsibility of the 136 head coaches and over 300 assistant coaches. The work that went into recruiting, selecting and training the

head coaches was well worth the effort. Over half of the 136 Schools of Sport were observed by either headquarters staff or the monitoring and evaluation team. The overwhelming response was that the sessions were just what we hoped they would be — exciting, well-organised, quality-controlled opportunities for young people wishing to build on their sporting abilities.

Well-qualified coaches who understand the importance of the craft involved in developing young players through their chosen sport are scarce. The second clearest lesson in Champion Coaching is that if we are to repeat and expand the project, we need to mobilise a whole army of people who can fill what was described as a gap twenty years ago in the Wolfenden report and is now becoming a void. It's a toss-up as to who has the greater need for signposts showing where to find after-school sport — the coaches or the children. Increasingly both are in the dark and perilously close to losing their way.

Let's not hold sport accountable for school-age successes and failures until we are clear about who is delivering what. We need to address the current differences in local sports provision by deciding what role the coaches should play in the overall sport experience of children aged 11 to 14. Is there one adult figure who organises and chaperones school teams in competition? Another who takes coaching sessions? Another who manages the child's junior league experience? And finally one who keeps a watchful eye on the performer as a county hopeful?

If the values and attitudes we ascribe to sport are to have any hope of germinating in young players, children must have attentive coaching from key role models who are informed about their total educational framework. Good coaching opportunities need structure, funding, coordination and a sound progression within single sports and across all sports.

Selecting the 6,000 children

No other variable in the Champion Coaching project was more hotly debated or interpreted so widely as child selection. National guidelines to the SLOs stated that performance skill-level was the

chief criterion for selection, but there were other factors too (see page 9). With few exceptions the children came to their Champion Coaching squad through the recommendation of their physical education teachers.

Many factors and constraints influenced local interpretation of the criteria. Here are some of them:

- Typically, schemes drew children from between 5 and 20 schools, spread across several districts, and pooled their most suitable youngsters into one squad. Understandably, the teachers did not all have the same definition of performance.

Result: Squads of mixed ability needed to be broken down into sub-groupings by experienced head coaches and assistant coaches. Exit routes including repeat sessions were organised to group the participants better the second time around.

- The schemes that wished to initiate girls' soccer often found it nearly impossible to recruit performance-standard players.

Result: Girls' soccer was conducted with eager and athletic young women who may have just been learning the game. The more experienced girls were used as peer coaches when appropriate.

- Champion Coaching strongly urged that the participants selected should be those who were not already receiving large doses of high-quality coaching.

Result: There was some difficulty in identifying children who were enthusiastic, had ability and were not already on a performance pathway. Head coaches and clubs worked together to assist schemes with this problem.

- Some schemes were inundated by requests for more sessions, because of family interest and the local and national momentum.

Result: Extra sessions were organised to meet the demand; often self-selection was relied upon in this repeat process.

Attendance and perceived value

The national attendance rate ran at approximately 87 per cent, even though many of the sports had to operate at outdoor venues in November and

December weather, and despite the problems of transport and mid-term breaks. Children saw Champion Coaching as a special opportunity to meet new friends, learn new skills and benefit from outstanding coaches. The review process of the children's *SportLogs* has begun in earnest, and preliminary findings show that the youngsters enjoyed their experience and want more of the same.

Facilities: where and why we chose the venues

Long-term provision for after-school sport will require all the venues in a community to be organised for effective use. A primary goal of Champion Coaching was to use the project to encourage partnerships between schools and the community. One way to do this was to request schemes that were school-based to include community facilities, and schemes that were community-based to seek out school facilities. Substantial time and energy had to be put into meeting this request, but the scheduling of safe and affordable facilities helped to create new awareness about local difficulties in organising after-school sport.

Putting together the pieces of a jigsaw which included facilities that had to be cost-effective from 4:00 pm to 6:00 pm, busy coaches who may have regular work until after 6:00 pm, and children who must be transported to and from the sites, was a most delicate exercise! The process required several networks to join together for the good of the whole community.

One of the critical issues for those desiring to direct school-age sport is the cost of facilities. Regardless of whether the SLO faced the Local Management of Schools ledger or the Compulsory Competitive Tendering reality, *most places for children to practise and play cost money.*

On average, the 24 schemes spent 38 per cent of their budgets on facilities that ranged from free use to over £40 per hour. This expense was more than any other part of Champion Coaching's local budget, including the cost of assistant coaches, transport and publicity put together. And this included using some

facilities which were free: this is not a feature which can be relied upon in future, as the tendency is more and more for charging to increase.

So the question must be asked and answered: 'Who is responsible for funding after-school sport?'. Overall, facilities account for a major part of the costs involved.

Health and safety

Champion Coaching had given careful thought to the safety aspects of the project, and the importance of health and safety was stressed throughout.

In the event, only three serious injuries occurred. Two of these happened during playing time: one broken arm and one broken finger.

The third injury was especially unfortunate. The Bristol scheme provided transport on an unusually large scale, with scores of buses, vans and taxis, and Dave Travis, the SLO, realised that despite all precautions there was a risk of a traffic accident. His premonition came true when a child was knocked down while crossing the road, having been dropped off by bus after a coaching session, and suffered a broken leg.

All three children were treated promptly and are making a good recovery.

Transport: how much is enough?

Depending on the demographics and individual community expectations, transport varied greatly. Some urban schemes did not feel the need to offer transport while other more rural schemes knew they would not have had any participants without intricate pick-up and drop-off routes. Across the schemes, buses, minivans, taxis and family car pools were used to transport youngsters to and from their coaching sessions.

If performance pathways are to be made available to every interested and deserving child in Britain, there must be safe transport to training sessions and competitions. Whose responsibility is it to provide this?

Exit routes: building for tomorrow

One of the more gratifying aspects of watching the Champion Coaching project grow and mature was observing the development of each scheme's design of exit routes for their children. Here are a few of the proposed avenues for continued coaching and competition:

● newly-created junior clubs housed in schools

● Leisure Services Departments providing directed programmes with extended age groups upward and downward from Champion Coaching's range of 11 to 14

● single-sport and multi-sport clubs making provision for Champion Coaching participants to join them

● individual coaches continuing sessions for interested children

● Champion Coaching scheme advisory groups budgeting for the continuation of sport sessions within their community networks

Spotting the talent

Britain's most talented young performers are usually picked up by sport-specific development officers or through other national governing body avenues. But what about the late bloomer, the slightly-less-than-county-standard performer or the keen all-round substitute to the school's first team? If 'Sport for All' is going to be more than a slogan hanging on leisure-centre walls, we must ensure that performance pathways exist for *all* our youngsters to reach their full potential in sport. They must have the opportunity to test themselves in appropriate competition, along with high-quality coaching, so that their youthful aptitudes can be encouraged and measured. Our current opportunities for children to make the transition from participation to performance need clearer signposts and an expanded road map.

The Minister for Sport, Robert Atkins MP, getting into the spirit of Champion Coaching during a tennis session at Maidenhead

Cost snapshot

The pie chart below shows the breakdown of the local budget averaged over the 24 schemes. The 'other' category included payment for PE planning time, additional coach education, sports science support, etc.

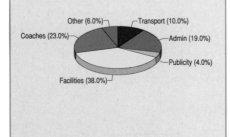

Other (6.0%)
Transport (10.0%)
Coaches (23.0%)
Admin (19.0%)
Publicity (4.0%)
Facilities (38.0%)

Lessons along the way

Although relatively short in duration, the project covered a lot of ground in terms of effort and resourcefulness. Along the way we learned and relearned a few overriding lessons which will form the basis for Champion Coaching's recommendations:

● Provision for after-school sport in England is currently very varied in quantity and quality. It is continuing to change because of current trends in legislation, funding, facility management, physical education and children's attitudes.

● There exists a group of local, regional and national networks which have an interest in delivering after-school sport. They are not currently coordinated, which causes a great deal of fragmentation and confusion. The main networks are physical education, national sport governing bodies, local authorities, the Sports Councils and the voluntary agencies.

● There is a strong will and determination to provide after-school sport, but putting partnerships into practice is extremely difficult. When each network perceives itself as operating primarily in its own interests, the partnership model for sport development becomes weakened.

● When given clear national direction and focus, the networks can and do work well together.

Clearly, one of the largest contributions Champion Coaching has made is to demonstrate the power of collaboration.

The project has been an impartial agency that guided a national sport development package for the benefit of children in local schemes. The effectiveness of the project relied on the fact that it was independent, could provide an open forum for debate, and had the remit to encourage partnership negotiation.

Champion Coaching has lifted the issues of after-school sport to a new level, establishing an innovative regional and national platform where the many networks involved could review the positive results of their working together in partnership.

A room with a view

Once or twice in a career one is privileged to be given the chance to seek higher ground. The Champion Coaching project allowed the headquarters team this kind of opportunity, and it was one which gave an unparalleled view of British after-school sport. From Bury to Bristol, from Carlisle to Eastbourne, we saw what is happening now and what is possible in the future.

The room from which we took this view was a plain office in a Leeds suburb. It was provided by the National Coaching Foundation, and supplied with just enough basic equipment to implement the scheme. Here was where Champion Coaching found the roots to grow and the wings to fly.

The light shed on the view came from the national networks we negotiated with, which helped to open the doors at local level. But gaining the higher ground was only possible through the collective climbing efforts of the 24 schemes all leading the way forward.

The Next Phase

Possibilities for future development

As we saw time and again when setting up the original Champion Coaching programme, the provision of after-school sport varies enormously from community to community.

With so many variables to contend with, and continued change on the horizon, what can we learn from one relatively small pilot project such as Champion Coaching? Have we really found a formula for a workable solution to a problem which has been around for a decade or more?

Maybe ...

The answer lies in collective vision and effort: by itself, each of the 24 schemes was a faint light illuminating only a limited area. Fused together and focused, these lights became an intense laser beam capable of joining communities together and producing common solutions.

A popular project

Although the 1991 Champion Coaching project could reach only 6.5 per cent of the 365 English local authorities, the central office in Leeds received letters from scores more that would have been pleased to join.

Likewise, from over a hundred possibilities, practical considerations allowed Champion Coaching to deliver only eleven different sports. However, as soon as the initial announcements were made, there was a constant stream of enquiries from the national governing bodies of other sports about how to be included in the next phase.

Variety and ingenuity

It can be argued that an excessive amount of time and resources went into jump-starting the machinery needed to deliver Champion Coaching to 6,000 children. However, this effort produced more than just the basic project. Nearly every scheme wrote a second phase of courses into its programme, as these examples show:

In Ryedale, RACE's proposal to Champion Coaching was written as a three-year endeavour, while Carlisle and Middlesbrough both ran two sets of their Schools of Sport. Some schemes served more than one centre of population, and of these, Blackburn/South Ribble, Windsor/Maidenhead and St Edmundsbury all ran Schools of Sport in each of their two major communities simultaneously. An ingenious approach was used in Northamptonshire and Nottinghamshire, where the first part of a two-phase Champion Coaching scheme served as a selection process for Schools of Excellence, involving over 1,200 children taking part in enthusiastic tournament 'playdays'.

In virtually every case, the communities hosting the project have made every effort to plan sensibly for life after Champion Coaching. Regardless of whether or not second-phase funding is available, the machinery to continue sound school-age sport development work is in place and turning over nicely.

Certainly, there is more work to be done with and for children in offering integrated Schools of Sport. But the unequivocal feedback from coaches, Scheme Liaison Officers, parents, teachers and children themselves is that they enjoyed Champion Coaching, they benefited from it and wish to repeat the experience. The project has had an enormous appeal for parents by making the whole subject of after-school sport simpler, more understandable and accessible.

We believe that Champion Coaching may have much to offer as an active 'research vehicle' which can turn current policies and principles into practice with a single purpose. It can enable partnerships to be negotiated in which national, regional and local networks understand their common mission, speak the same language and mobilise the appropriate decision-makers.

Respecting the past

It is important to acknowledge that numerous examples of good practice in after-school sport existed across the country long before Champion Coaching was conceived. There is a long-standing tradition of teachers working in conventional school sport through a variety of associations. For a long time, too, individual national governing bodies have provided a variety of opportunities such as junior proficiency awards, residential schools, and local, regional and national excellence schemes.

There are areas of the country where the traditional school model of sport is alive and doing well. Champion Coaching recognised both the established and the innovative systems, and relied heavily on each in our schemes.

Communication

Accepting the role as one of after-school sport's honest brokers has been an enormous undertaking with serious responsibilities. In Phase One, Champion Coaching reached out to the physical education profession, to the Sports Council regional offices, to local authorities, to the national governing bodies, to the Central Council of Physical Recreation, to the National Council for Schools Sports, and to various volunteer agencies (linked with the National Council for Voluntary Youth Services). In many cases Champion Coaching built on the good practice already in place and was primarily seeking the understanding and goodwill of the various organisations involved. They were simply invited to join in the dream of a nationally coordinated, quality-controlled, after-school sport strategy for children aged 11–14.

Less than a year later, the dream is most certainly alive and well: it has become a working reality with real benefits. The criteria for full involvement are becoming clear, and we have gained the collective experience to articulate what each network's expanded role must become for increased success.

How might a Phase Two proceed? We think that the first step is to improve communication with and between all the main networks that have a stake in the direction which after-school sport will take. Criteria for full membership of Champion Coaching, and the benefits that membership will bring, must be clearly spelled out.

Already a start has been made: we have had discussion meetings with the main networks and associations to begin formulating their possible roles, to spell out the benefits and to shape management targets at all levels.

Identifying the variables

Champion Coaching's quality-controlled after-school sport model is potentially capable of expanding in a number of ways in Phase Two:

- By increasing the number of sports — working in partnership with national governing bodies to ensure greater national, regional and local support

- By increasing the number of schemes to include other agencies and organisations that meet the criteria and that are willing to go the extra mile to promote sound sport development

- By developing sports programmes for children in each school term, with avenues to appropriate competitions, so that there are year-round competitive opportunities to test the skills learned and also to live out Champion Coaching's fair-play education

- By increasing education and training for everybody in the sporting community who works with children — coaches, officials and administrators

- By producing appropriate job descriptions for Youth Sport Coordinators and other personnel involved in after-school sport

- By involving and educating a larger number of parents in all aspects of the project

- By creating advisory groups drawn from all the agencies involved in after-school sport to work with and assist each Youth Sport Coordinator (as recommended in *Sport and Young People: Partnership and Action*).

- By enabling physical education students to take coaching practice placements in Champion Coaching Schools of Sport

- By planning some of the Champion Coaching Schools of Sport so that they provide opportunities for the assessment of coaching competence for candidates on NVQ courses

In developing after-school sport, it's sometimes necessary to move the goal-posts — but only with the consent of all the agencies involved ...

Our initial charge was, quite specifically, to increase opportunities for good quality after-school sport for children aged 11–14. That is still our prime responsibility. Only after we have assured ourselves and our networks that we can continue to deliver top-notch sporting experiences for children and coaches will additional features be added. Trial ingredients will not be implemented at the expense of our fundamental mission.

Applications to run schemes

After the main national networks have been confirmed and the 1992–93

Champion Coaching agenda has been set, applications will be accepted for entry into Phase Two. It is anticipated that invitations to apply will go out to all local authorities and interested agencies who wish to collaborate.

Successful applicants must be able to deliver the nuts and bolts of the scheme, and preference will be shown to partners who have really positive ideas about the direction of after-school sport for children.

Champion Coaching Phase Two will seek partnership with agencies which are willing to channel their own resources wholeheartedly into this exciting and dynamic initiative for sport in the United Kingdom.

The long-term vision

Champion Coaching Phase One, against what some critics thought would be heavy odds and an impossible timescale, survived and thrived to provide after-school sport for 6,000 young people. The lessons that were learned and re-learned allow a look into the future: please turn the page ...

The year is 2001

As we travel into the year 2001, let us try to imagine what may be possible if we have been successful in motivating people in many networks to be *pro-active*, to take initiatives to consult and work together effectively.

Many areas of youth sport might now look quite different:

Coaching

Coaches have participated in producing agreed national standards for all coaches

who work with children. There is a national register of qualified coaches working with children which is accessible to all potential employers.

Champion Coaching has helped to raise the profile of coaches, and many more now work as part-time and full-time employees in after-school sport. Consistent minimum pay-scales are in place for those with accepted qualifications.

A growing number of master coaches act as mentors to novice coaches working with children, all of them operating to an agreed national code of practice.

Overall, the role of the coach in after-school sport is more clearly understood, appreciated and valued throughout the worlds of sport and education.

Physical education

By 2001, the role of teachers in after-school sport has been re-evaluated. Changes have taken place in initial teacher-training; these include the introduction of a range of educational modules which equip teachers to:

- interpret the National Curriculum effectively
- manage school sports facilities effectively so that they accommodate after-school sport programmes along with other community use
- become pro-active sports development workers, often leading the way rather than following others
- understand performance development through increasing their coaching knowledge and skills.

During their training, it is usual for student-teachers to be given placements in schools, clubs, sports development units, Champion Coaching schemes and national governing body coaching schemes.

In-service training opportunities are run jointly by physical education departments and sports development units, thus ensuring greater exchange of information and sharing of knowledge.

National governing bodies develop sports curricula in consultation with physical education organisations for use both inside and outside school.

As the new century starts, the physical education profession is again one of the key agencies in after-school sport provision, and the morale and status of physical education teachers is much improved.

Parents

Throughout the 1990s, the steady implementation of a nationally conducted programme of parent workshops has encouraged families to be much more involved in after-school sport. They have become a political force to be reckoned with, concerned with both the quality of coaching and the importance of fair play in their children's after-school sport.

More parents have entered the lower tiers of coaching and are receiving the appropriate coach education.

National parent groups have produced a parents' code of practice within sport.

On a practical level, parents have put increasing effort into:

- Operating car pools to transport the children to sessions
- Fund-raising for equipment and for training scholarships
- Management of schools, putting physical education and sport high on the agenda.

Head teachers and governors

Head teachers and governors are now much more involved in after-school sport, and there is a greater overall commitment to physical education and sport both within the school curriculum and in extra-curricular time. The implementation of nationally conducted workshops in sport and physical education has played a big part in this. School managements appreciate the importance of sport on student enrolment when marketing schools to young people and their families.

There is more appreciation of the need for joint use of facilities, and a growing awareness that these facilities can generate income if marketed well. Therefore head teachers and governors are investing more heavily in facilities and equipment.

The prestige of the schools has improved because they have also invested in the personnel — teachers and coaches — who can deliver high-quality coaching to children within the established educational environment.

Youth Sport Coordinators

Since Champion Coaching first publicised the vital role that Youth Sport Coordinators (YSCs) play, national guidelines for their employment have evolved. These include:

- Specimen job descriptions
- Standard conditions of service

- Recommendations for minimum rates of pay
- Assessment criteria
- Ethical controls
- Evaluation procedures

By 2001, Youth Sport Coordinators are routinely involved in the national development of policy and practice in after-school sport.

A National Association of Youth Sport Coordinators has been set up, providing employment placement services, in-service training, continuing education and training, a newsletter and an annual conference.

Local authorities

For ten years now, Champion Coaching has acted as a catalyst in developing local strategies for improved and expanded after-school sport. These local coaching strategies, introduced by all local authorities, have increased community awareness about the importance of coaching in after-school sport. The Youth Sport Coordinators and their advisory groups have played a major part in achieving this.

Quality-control measures are now applied, to ensure that only coaches and YSCs from the national register are employed.

Most local authorities are working through their sport development units to maintain local coaching registers and to run coach education courses for their communities.

Guidelines for sports facility use now include providing time and opportunity for young people, and when new leisure facilities are planned, the extent to which they will serve the school population is automatically taken into consideration. Increasingly, the sporting talents of Britain's young in the twenty-first century are nurtured in pleasant, clean surroundings — a contrast to the often makeshift arrangements of earlier days.

YSCs and their advisory committees now play an important part in helping local authorities to manage and coordinate their after-school sport personnel.

National governing bodies of sport

Most national governing bodies (NGBs) now recognise the importance of after-school sport: they devote a significant part of their resources to it, and promote the training of officials for youth sport much more energetically than in the past.

After working with Champion Coaching on multi-sport schemes, the NGBs have established minimum standards for coaches working in after-school sport.

Because of the need to produce accurate coaching registers for hundreds of Champion Coaching Schools of Sport, NGBs have developed an appropriate administrative structure for youth sport.

The NGBs' numerous sport development officers have been coordinated to make them more effective in delivering after-school sport to young people.

Competitive structures have been developed which integrate sound coaching, training and matches, while also keeping fair-play education high on the agenda. Appropriate skill awards schemes are available nationally for all children.

Sports Council

The voices lobbying central government about the value of after-school sport are much stronger, and the government has been willing to establish long-term funding for nationally coordinated schemes through the new UK Sports Commission.

The Sports Councils have modified both their financial and their ethical priorities to put after-school sport at the top of the list. This has also influenced many other agencies to give greater emphasis to the subject. A national information service for youth sport has been established. At the heart of this is a monitoring and evaluation department for all youth sport projects.

The Sports Councils have invested in widespread incentives to refurbish and upgrade school sports facilities. Incentives for dual use of facilities, with guidelines to ensure that performance sport for children gets adequate time, have been particularly effective.

The children

Over half a million children have experienced the Champion Coaching project as it has grown and matured during its first ten years. They now have many more sports with high-quality coaching available to them.

In 2001, children have far greater opportunities to participate in sport at all levels. They know where to go to take part, whether they wish to keep fit, meet friends or to excel — and those wishing to reach for the stars have a route map to get there.

As the twenty-first century starts, children are having fun in sport as never before. If only the future were now ...

'The greatest danger in life is not taking the risk to excel.'

George Mallory

INDEX

Major page references are given in **bold**
type.